G. H Stockham

Temperance and Prohibition

G. H Stockham

Temperance and Prohibition

ISBN/EAN: 9783743302747

Manufactured in Europe, USA, Canada, Australia, Japa

Cover: Foto ©ninafisch / pixelio.de

Manufactured and distributed by brebook publishing software (www.brebook.com)

G. H Stockham

Temperance and Prohibition

TEMPERANCE

AND

PROHIBITION.

BY

G. H. STOCKHAM, M. D.

"We love no triumphs sprung of force,
They stain the brightest cause."

OAKLAND, CAL.:
PUBLISHED BY THE AUTHOR.
1888.

Entered according to Act of Congress, in the year 1888, by

G. H. STOCKHAM, M. D.

In the Office of the Librarian of Congress, at Washington.

ALL RIGHTS RESERVED

PACIFIC PRESS PUBLISHING CO.,
PRINTERS, ELECTROTYPERS AND BINDERS,
Twelfth and Castro Sts, Oakland, Cal.

PREFACE.

HAVING been a contemporary of the Rev. Theobald Mathew during the great temperance movement originated by him, we were deeply interested in his work. Though but a youth at the time, the recollections of this extraordinary man are still vivid in our mind. We witnessed the wonderful enthusiasm that attended his labors in Dublin, and being then a resident of that city were present at many of his lectures.

We remained in Ireland long enough afterwards also to witness the relapsing of the people into their former habits of inebriety, and the gradual decline of the temperance lodges.

For the last three decades we have watched with continued interest the progress of the cause in America, and have seen with regret the failure of all license and prohibitory laws to crush out the leviathan of intemperance. The contemplation of this matter in its divers bearings on the welfare of humanity, led to our devoting what time we could spare from professional duties during the past few months to a closer study of the subject. Finding so much to interest and instruct as we advanced in our investigations, we conceived the plan of arranging certain facts and data into articles for publication. But as the matter grew on our hands we abandoned our first idea as being wholly inadequate to the setting forth of a subject that had now assumed enlarged proportions in our own mind.

If the result of this labor be received with favor, it will be most gratifying; but, on the other hand, if it meet adverse criticism, and thereby fail of its object, we shall at least have the consolation of having simply fulfilled what, to us, seemed a duty.

G. H. STOCKHAM.

Oakland, April, 1888.

CONTENTS.

CHAPTER.		PAGE.
	Preface.....	3
I.	Origin of the Temperance Movement..........	7
II.	Temperance Societies	11
III.	The Origin and History of Wine..............	15
IV.	The History and Properties of Beer...........	19
V.	History and Constituents of Spirituous Liquors.	23
VI.	The Adulteration of Liquors.................	26
VII.	Comparative Effects of Fermented and Spirituous Liquors.............................	32
VIII.	Physiological Action of Alcohol..............	36
IX.	Alcohol as Food...........................	44
X.	Alcohol as a Medicine and a Poison....	50
XI.	Alcohol as a Stimulant and a Narcotic	54
XII.	Licensing Systems of Great Britain and America.	57
XIII.	American Liquor Laws and Local Option......	66
XIV.	Sumptuary Laws...........................	73
XV.	Prohibition	79
XVI.	Causes of Intemperance.	91
XVII.	Remedies Suggested for Intemperance.........	97
XVIII.	Advantages of an Increased Production of Wine and Beer	106
XIX.	Alcohol as a Factor in Human Progress........	113
XX.	To Prohibitionists..........................	121

CHAPTER I.

ORIGIN OF THE TEMPERANCE MOVEMENT.

The modern temperance movement began in the city of Cork, Ireland, in the year 1838, by the Rev. Theobald Mathew, commonly called "Father Mathew, the Apostle of Temperance." The great moral reformation, principally brought about by his instrumentality, both in its immediate and subsequent results, was unexampled in history. He was the first Roman Catholic clergyman who attained prominence in Ireland as a temperance reformer. Father Mathew was a man of singular purity and simplicity of character, with an utter unselfishness that made him dearly beloved by all the people.

A few years prior to 1838 he commenced preaching in the temperance cause, and the same year formulated a pledge which he urged all his hearers to sign. It ran as follows: "I promise to abstain from all intoxicating drinks, except those used medicinally, and by order of a physician; and to discontinue the cause and practice of intemperance."

During that year, 1838, the roads were thronged with people hastening to declare their total abandonment of drink, and before its close, one hundred and fifty thousand signatures from Cork and its surrounding country, were added to the pledge. The excitement was intense. Good men of all denominations joined his heroic labors. A great improvement was brought about in general morals, and in a stricter observance of law and order in entire communities. The police force had little to do. Lawyers were without briefs, and criminal judges had few cases on their dockets. So eager were the converts to the new dispensation that many traveled one hundred miles to sign the pledge and receive the blessing of the good Father. All classes, Catholic, Protestant, and Dissenters, upheld him in his work. It was estimated that during seven or eight days in Dublin as many as sixty thousand persons joined this temperance movement; and in the short space of two days, one hundred thousand in Galway added their names to swell the ranks. By November, in 1844, Father Mathew had registered upwards of 5,000,000 adherents of total abstinence principles in Ireland.

After a few years' experience, it was found advisable to alter the wording of the pledge to the following formula: "I solemnly promise with the divine assistance, as long as I continue a member of the 'Teetotal Temperance Society,' to abstain from all intoxicating drinks, except for medicinal and sacramental purposes, and I will do everything in my power, by advice and example, to discontinue drunkenness." This, it will be seen, carried an essentially different meaning than was indorsed in the former document; anyone who found himself unable to keep the pledge could preserve his self-respect by returning it to the society.

The moral regeneration brought about by Father Mathew's work was most astonishing and gratifying to every philanthropic mind. It continued to increase in popularity, and practical reforms were set up on every hand. Coffee shops took the place of whisky saloons and thrived as well as the latter had formerly done. The excise revenue of Ireland was reduced from upwards of $5,000,000 to less than half that sum. Father Mathew extended his labors into England and the United States, meeting with universal appreciation in both these countries, and was hailed by all classes as a public benefactor. In all the cities visited he left behind him temperance lodges in a flourishing condition. To many minds the movement was the ushering in of a new era in the history of man. They believed that King Alcohol was dethroned and overpowered, and to Ireland was accorded the honor of being more temperate than either England or Scotland. Statistics showed that the sale of whisky there was reduced to three-fourths its former estimate. The work progressed gloriously for some years, but with nations, as with individuals in any of the relations of life, undue excitement cannot be perpetuated *ad infinitum*, but must sooner or later be followed by a subsequent reaction or depression. So it proved with the temperance reformation. People became less vigorous in the observance of their pledge, and many withdrew from the societies and gradually fell back into old habits of inebriety. It was not long before there was as much intoxicating liquor sold and drunk as before the noble efforts of Father Mathew. This generous friend of humanity, assisted by faithful members of the temperance lodges, did all he could to stay this downward course; but one by one they were overcome by the strong current of human life that finally returned to its old channel. Thus ended the greatest temperance movement ever inagurated, and though it failed in its object to permanently rescue the people from the slavery of intoxicating drinks, yet it left a lasting influence behind, and to-day men have reason to thank God for the existence of such a man as the Rev. Theobald Mathew.

If the temperance reform did not cure, it undoubtedly palliated the evil it attempted to subvert. The cause had become popular with all classes, whether among the rich in their palaces, or the poor in their lowly dwellings. It had been an almost universal practice with those who could afford it, to keep various kinds of liquors in their houses, and it was considered a breach of hospitality and good manners to allow a visitor to go away without being invited to partake of some one of these refreshments. The sideboard was never without its arrangement of glasses and decanters of carefully selected brands of wine, whisky and brandy, which were served according to the taste of each guest. During the excitement this custom was discontinued, and it has never been renewed to any extent down to the present day. The banishment of a practice that extended not only over the United Kingdom of Great Britain and Ireland, but also that of the United States of America, was probably the greatest good affected by this reformation of the Rev. Theobald Mathew.

CHAPTER II.

TEMPERANCE SOCIETIES.

AFTER a few years of inaction the cause of temperance was revived. Lodges were resuscitated and new ones organized. Able men and women, too, entered the lecture field. The people were again interested. The lodges worked with increased vigor, and many a poor inebriate was, for the time being, raised from the gutter. Much good was undoubtedly done, but it was principally by individual exertion. The moderate drinker and the habitual drunkard, however, still took their liquors. The efforts of the most earnest speakers made no lasting impression on the public mind. Still the work progressed. Temperance societies continued to be established locally and spasmodically, and everything possible was done by honest enthusiasts to stop the traffic in the accursed thing. But the sad fact remained that saloons multiplied, and the average amount of spirituous liquors sold in proportion to the population, was even greater than before. The receipts of the tax collector showed that the number of persons addicted to habits of intemperance, had increased rather than diminished; that comparatively few drunkards had been reclaimed, thus proving the inherent weakness of the lodges. Something wrong in their very constitution must account for this inability to successfully cope with this hydra-headed evil.

The temperance societies commit an error in waging war equally against moderate drinkers and those who are confirmed drunkards. The former enjoy their glass of wine or beer at dinner, or even a little toddy, and do not admit the justice of a law that compels them to sacrifice this, to them, harmless practice, for the sake of the inebriate.

When a pledge is broken it implies a want of honor, veracity, and firmness of character; and a man who has done this, feels at once not only his dishonor in the eyes of the lodge, but, what is much worse, the inevitable loss of his own self-respect. Few have the will-power to keep, for any length of time, a pledge that is against inclination and the sanction of custom. The person who withdraws from the lodge is esteemed hardly less blamable than he who has violated the pledge. He has evinced a changeableness of opinion that warrants the conclusion of weakness of character and general unreliability. He is under a sort of social ban afterwards.

Any law is bad in its tendencies when it interferes with the free agency and moral responsibility of man. It is setting aside the divine right of conscience and reason to guide and control the individual. Every contest of the soul determines his spiritual status. One is either stronger or weaker after the battle, for this eternal warfare is but a necessary development of character, a bringing out of the possibilities of the soul. When a man voluntarily binds himself to an oath he has surrendered his individuality. He is no longer free, for he is bound in the chains of another's forging. The question has ceased to be open to him as a moral, rational, accountable being. He is under restraint or authority. After a season he begins to chafe at his loss of freedom, and realizes with impatience that fetters are not so easily broken as forged. He is even tempted to hypocrisy and takes his dram in secret. His temptation to drink is rather increased than diminished by this imposed bond to "touch not, taste not." He becomes daily more irritated because he cannot openly take a social glass with his companions, and feels that his business interests have suffered thereby; it is not pleasant to one's friends to constantly refuse to drink with them. The result is too often the breaking of his pledge and a wretched after-feeling of having justly lost the respect of himself and his associates.

Temperance societies will be obliged to go farther back than the individual to effect a reformation that will be permanent and universal. They must begin with a regeneration of the laws governing society. We generally find an excuse for doing what we most desire to do. An oath or promise, verbal or written, does not quench insatiable thirst, destroy passion or the internal desire for what we see no particular harm in using. People must be educated up to a law, before it can be enforced. The convert to temperance societies is usually gained under a temporary excitement which implies the influence of passion. Now, passion is always fatal to principle and philosophy. Large numbers of people are seldom at the same time inspired by principle, and a universal conversion of a multitude to philosophy is an impossibility. Philosophers never unite in large bodies. We must not, however, be accused of doing an injustice to the temperance societies, whose devotion, energy, and usefulness cannot be too highly extolled. They have undoubtedly done, and are still doing, a grand work with the young, in training them to habits of temperance and a high regard for the interests of others. The unanimity of sentiment among the members has been a strong means of mutual aid and support, and the rising generation have reason to be grateful for these societies.

To better comprehend the main subjects involved in this work, it will be necessary to give a short synopsis of the history of fermented and spirituous liquors, and their relative effects on the human system.

CHAPTER III.

THE ORIGIN AND HISTORY OF WINE.

The manufacture of wine may be considered as almost coeval with the production of the grape. That the Creator designed its use seems as evident as that bread should be made from wheat. Nor are we without scriptural authority for this statement. The country given over to the Jews by divine command was distinguished by the productiveness of its vineyards; and the wine manufactured therefrom was counted as one of the choicest gifts bestowed on them by the Lord. As a punishment for disobedience, wine was withheld from the people; while, on the other hand, an abundance of this article was regarded as the shadowing forth of a blessing. That this highly commended drink was then as now the *fermented* juice of the grape, no competent judge will deny. The scriptural evidence of this fact, both direct and indirect, is too strong to admit of disputation. It is recorded that God not only legislated for the Jews in things religious, but also taught them what they should eat and drink. The conclusion is unavoidable that if wine was once legitimately used, it should yet be esteemed a blessing and not a curse. The first mention in history of this beverage is to be found in the Old Testament. That other nations beside the Jews employed this drink, we have proof positive. All races of men inhabiting southern climates converted their grapes into wine, and drank it daily in sobriety and thankfulness of heart. Thus from the earliest time we can trace the production of wine down through the generations to the present day. The cultivation of the grape is not now confined to narrow strips of country in Asia and Africa, but has gradually extended throughout Europe until the latter country has by far the greatest extent of vineyards in the world. The immensity of the wine industry makes it difficult to comprehend what becomes of such vast supplies of this product. France stands at the head of the wine-producing countries, and her output, before the ravages of the phylloxera, has often exceeded 2,500,000,000 gallons, but later her average is estimated to be about 1,450,000,000. Italy's vine-clad hills furnish 700,000,000 gallons, while Spain follows with her 580,000,000; Austria and Hungary, 375,000,000; Portugal, 132,000,000; Germany, 100,000,000; Russia, 53,000,000, and Greece, Servia, Turkey in Europe and the other European countries, have an average of 150,000,000 gallons. Wine is also manufactured in Asiatic Turkey, India, China, Japan, Arabia and Africa, and in fact in every locality where the climate and soil are favorable. Of late years it has become an important industry in the United States, especially in California, which will ultimately rival France as the greatest wine-producing country of the world. Already in the Eastern States and in Mexico, California wines are displacing those of France. The extraordinary growth and fruitage of the vine in this

State warrant us in speaking thus confidently of her future possibilities.

Wines are generally divided into two classes: First, those containing the pure juice of the grape, which are called natural wines, and second, those which have been fortified with spirits. The pure varieties, after having undergone a thorough fermentation, are seldom liable to further change. Such wines are therefore wholesome and of good keeping quality. On the other hand, in those which have been fortified, fermentation has not been allowed to run its regular course, having been prematurely checked by the addition of spirits. By this process its strength is brought above the limit within which vinous fermentation is possible.

Wines have two other divisions, white wines and red wines. Certain European districts produce the one, and certain other districts the other. It has been noticed as a remarkable fact that intemperance is more prevalent in all those localities where white wine is produced than in those that manufacture the red variety; and yet there is the same proportion of alcohol in each. So apparent is this that some employers import the red wine rather than allow their men to use the white product of the country. This difference is accounted for on the hypothesis that the former is rich in tannin, which, by its astringent properties, prevents the rapid absorption of the liquid; while the white, having little or no tannin, is quickly carried to the brain. There is also a theory that those who largely employ the uncolored wine rarely attain old age.

Owing to the phylloxera in France, certain parties

have lately patented a process for manufacturing both varieties of wine out of the red and white beets. The liquor obtained therefrom is said to possess all the properties of grape juice and is treated similarly. In England, currant, raspberry, and gooseberry wines are extensively employed for domestic purposes, and are highly prized as useful and beneficial adjuncts.

The relative amount of alcohol contained in wines is estimated at from 17 to 23 per cent in port, sherry and Madeira, $12\frac{1}{2}$ per cent in champagne, and from 7 to 11 per cent in other varieties.

CHAPTER IV.

THE HISTORY AND PROPERTIES OF BEER.

UNDER this heading we include ale and porter, which, like beer, is made from barley and hops, by a process of fermentation similar to that used in the manufacture of wines. The brewing of malt liquor was known many hundred years before the Christian era. It was employed by the ancient Egyptians, Greeks, Romans and Gauls, and has an unbroken lineage down to the present day. It was discovered about the same time as the production of wine from the grape.

Commercial beer is chiefly made from barley, which is first malted and ground and its fermentable substance extracted by warm water. Afterwards it is evaporated by boiling, and hops added to effect its preservation. Although ale and porter come under the general name of beer, being equally a product of brewing, yet there is a difference in taste, color and amount of alcohol contained in them. Small beer is a pleasant drink and has little alcohol, not more than 1.28 per cent, while Burton and Edinburgh ales contain from 6 to 8 per cent. The German brewers make a distinction between their ale and beer on account of the different modes of fermentation employed. In manufacturing the former, rapid fermentation is produced, thus causing the yeast to rise to the surface;

while in making beer a slower process is used, which compels the yeast to settle to the bottom of the cask.

The term "lager bier" is indiscriminately applied in this country to any light kind of beer prepared by this slow fermentation. Much, however, of this beverage is not the genuine "lager," it not having lain a sufficient length of time in the cellar to acquire that title; nor could it be preserved in casks during the time in which lager beer is ripening. This quality is known to the brewers as draught beer. It contains less alcohol than is found in genuine lager, and occupies less time in fermenting, though it has not the keeping properties of German lager. In the latter, after the liquid has attained a certain degree of fermentation, it is drawn off into large casks and allowed to remain for several months in cool cellars, which are kept at a temperature between 40° and 50° Fahr. A fining process here continues and the beer becomes perfectly transparent and free from all fermentable matter. Enormous quantities of ice are used in these cellars to equalize the temperature.

A few years ago a report was circulated that strychnine was employed in the manufacture of beer; this is an impossibility. It cannot be introduced into ordinary beer, as hops refuse to take up a single particle of it, or, for that matter, many other noxious drugs besides strychnine. They are entirely precipitated by the infusion of that wholesome herb.

Porter was made first in England in 1730. Previous to that time the only malt liquors in England were ale and beer. A portion of the malt used porter is roasted to a certain degree, thus giving a deeper color to this liquor.

Beer is the national drink of all those countries that are too cold for the grape, England and Germany more especially. In the former country it is stated that the capital invested in this industry amounts to $585,000,000; the number of persons employed in, and dependent upon, this traffic, 1,500,000; the quantity of liquor brewed in 1869, 25,542,664 barrels, and the revenue derived by the British Government, $60,000,000.

In 1871 the amount of beer manufactured in Austria and Hungary was 8,549,371 barrels. The German States, including Bavaria, Wurtenberg and Baden, produced from January to May in 1872, 3,733,769 barrels, and the year before in the same length of time, Bavaria alone went as high as 4,285,000 barrels. In the United States it is assuming colossal proportions; in 1879 the amount brewed was estimated at 7,179,760 barrels; in 1886, upwards of 20,000,000 barrels of thirty-one gallons each, on which the Government tax was in the neighborhood of $19,000,000.

It is a curious fact that the English nation do not consume half as much beer as they did in the reign of Queen Anne. The average consumption from 1740 to 1790, a period of fifty years, as compared with the same length of time between 1821 and 1871, is as 380 for the former to 150 for the latter. It is believed that the introduction of tea accounts in a measure for this decrease. Formerly beer was drunk at every meal and at frequent intervals during the day.

Now, the people use enormous quantities of tea, averaging about four pounds per head per annum. Beer has a proportion of alcohol ranging from $1\frac{1}{4}$ per cent in small beer to Burton ale, which averages about 8 per cent.

CHAPTER V.

HISTORY AND CONSTITUENTS OF SPIRITUOUS LIQUORS.

UNDER this head we class all alcoholic beverages produced by the process of distillation. The art of separating alcoholic spirit from fermented liquors appears to have been known, as in the case of wine and beer, from remote antiquity. It is supposed to have been discovered and practiced by the Chinese, who obtained alcohol from rice. From them a knowledge of the art traveled westward. In the twelfth century, when Henry II. invaded and conquered Ireland, the inhabitants were in the habit of making and using an alcoholic liquor similar to the whisky now drunk, which they called "usquabagh" or "potteen."

All substances in nature which contain sugar in any of its forms, are susceptible of vinous fermentation, and consequently may be considered as sources of alcohol. There is an endless variety of organic substances, more especially in the vegetable kingdom, from which alcohol can be extracted. Uncivilized races distill it from various trees, plants, and fruits and also from milk; but however obtained the spirit found in the product has the same chemical constituents. The spirituous liquors most commonly manufactured in this country and in Europe, are brandy, rum and whisky. Genuine brandy in France is made from wine. Rum, which is produced from molasses or treacle, is principally distilled in the West Indies; while whisky, in America and the British Isles, is manufactured from fermented infusions of grain. By adding the necessary flavoring ingredients to whisky, gin is made. In France, Germany, and Russia, what is termed "potato spirit," is extensively prepared from the tuber from which it derives its name, and is much used for fortifying wines.

The Irish brands of whisky are made almost exclusively from barley. Varieties of brandy are produced from different fruits, and owe to them their distinctive flavor and names, being familiarly known as "peach brandy," "apple brandy," etc.

Most ardent spirits contain fusil oil, which gives them a burning taste. It is found in nearly all whiskies, particularly in those made from Indian corn and potatoes. This oil unites with alcohol in all proportions, but has little affinity for water, for which reason it cannot be diluted. Fusil oil acts upon the coating of the stomach as an irritant poison, and is the principal cause of that dreadful disease, *mania a potu*, or delirium tremens. It may be detected by agitating the liquor with water and leaving it to stand for the oil to rise to the surface.

New spirits are not fit for internal use, and should not be placed upon the market until their constituent elements are thoroughly combined by age, and the fusil oil has had time to be more or less eliminated. For the purpose of producing a kind of artificial age various contrivances have been adopted in this and foreign countries. A variety of compounds are used to accomplish this result, which have to a certain extent been successful.

In 1876 the consumption of alcoholic liquors in England was 23,824.890 gallons, affording an internal revenue tax of nearly $100,000,000. In the same year Russia consumed 60,500,000 gallons. In France in 1885 it reached nearly 48,000,000. In the United States the revenue derived from this source in 1884 was about $80,000,000. In Germany and Italy the income from the taxation of liquors is comparatively small, as the vice of drunkenness has never attained serious proportions in these countries.

What is called "proof spirit" contains about equal proportions of alcohol and water by weight, being 49.24 parts of the former and 50.76 of the latter, the atomic weight of alcohol standing as 0.794, to 1.00 of water. Rum, whisky, brandy and gin have a general average of from 53 to 57 per cent of alcohol. Drinking spirits are seldom sold over .11 above proof, from which it varies downward to 25 under proof. Rum, however, is manufactured and imported as highly concentrated as from 10 to 45 over proof.

CHAPTER VI.

THE ADULTERATION OF LIQUORS.

We have collected from the works of Hassel and other authors many of the facts on adulteration of liquors contained in this chapter. The aggregate is certainly startling and merits the thoughtful consideration of every well-wisher of the human race. Eminent chemists assert that nine-tenths of all the liquor used in the United States, is more or less poisoned by drugs. There are thousands of men to-day that are thriving financially on this nefarious business.

A variety of articles are employed in these adulterations, some of which are sugar of lead, capsicum, juniper berries, aloes, logwood, verdigris, etc., according to the liquor to be simulated. Cheap whisky is converted into *best* cognac brandy; champagne, old port, sherry, in fact all wines are so closely imitated as to make it difficult for an expert to detect the difference. In the United States more port wine is drunk in one year than passes through the Custom House in ten; and the same proportion of champagne is used above what the entire district of Champagne produces. The failure of the whole crop of Madeira causes no apparent diminution of the quantity in the market; and the price of cognac brandy is four times as high in France as it is here. If other proof than chemical analysis were needed to establish the fact of the universal adulteration of liquors, it is found in the above statement. It is the presence of these poisonous compounds that ruins the health of such multitudes of people, and tends to excite them to all manner of crimes.

As before observed the inhabitants of Ireland drink far less whisky to-day than previous to the advent of Rev. Theobald Mathew; yet a case of delirium tremens was seldom known to them then, though in the present day it is a common occurrence. Since the *art of multiplication* by adulteration has achieved such prominence, this dread disease is now prevalent in all whisky-drinking countries. Owing to these spurious liquors intemperance has become so common in France that the Government has appointed a commission to investigate its cause. Just in the ratio that the manufacture of pure wine decreases, with a corresponding raise in its price, the introduction of adulteration takes place in any country. The demand is so great that if only good liquor were sold its enhanced value would place it beyond the reach of the majority, who consume the cheap, adulterated article. Admitting this, one of the most cogent and successful means to prevent intemperance would be legislation against the manufacture of spurious liquors, with a severe penalty attached for those found guilty of its infringement. The adoption of such a law would compel the support of whole communities, because it would not curtail the rights of any one individual, or render valueless any property except the implements and substances used for the purpose of adulterations. This law would be in harmony with our constitution and could therefore be enforced. Prohibitionists would greatly advance their cause by agitating this question.

It may be a matter of interest to the reader to give a few recipes commonly used in the adulteration of liquors. The peculiar flavor of true brandy is produced by the volatile oil of the grape and is simulated as follows: Take 100 gallons of alcohol and add half a pound of cream of tartar, a few gallons of French wine vinegar, a bushel or so of plums, the refuse of wine casks, half a bushel of oak sawdust, and a trifle of acetic ether, with the help of steam to give the combination head.

Another adulteration: Take 100 gallons of corn whisky, twelve gallons of spirit distilled from raisins, four gallons extract of paradise seed, two gallons of cherry laurel water, two gallons spirit almond cake, one-half bushel of oak sawdust, with the same steaming process as the other. In like manner all the better varieties of wines are imitated, and passed off on the public as the genuine article.

The following is a copy of a private circular lately sent to liquor dealers, and speaks for itself: "The undersigned would call the attention of manufacturers of liquors and wines to his very large stock of cognac oils, extracts of brandy, Holland and London gin, essence of rum, peach and cherry brandy, oils of rye for producing a superior Monongahela or Bourbon whisky from common corn spirit, and his invaluable preparations for neutralizing and giving age and body to new liquors. He has determined to reduce the price of all his goods, yet he warrants his oils to be superior to any other in this country. He guarantees to produce six barrels of good merchantable brandy from one ounce of cognac oil. Cherry juice and malva coloring for the manufacture of port wine, flavorings for ginger, claret, Madeira and Malaga wines, onanthic, acetic, and nitrous ethers, essential oils of almonds, juniper, caraway, rose, angelica, calamus, anise, absinthe, apple, pear, vanilla, raspberry, strawberry, pine-apple and banana, all of the best quality. The price will be satisfactory. Address, etc., etc.

PRICE CURRENT.

	Per oz.	Per lb.
Best Cognac Oil, 1 ounce to 6 barrels	$8 00	$100 00
Second Quality Cognac Oil, 1 ounce to 4 barrels....	6 00	50 00
Third Quality Cognac Oil, 1 ounce to 2 barrels....	3 00	25 00
Extract Cognac, 1 pound to 5 barrels..		10 00
Oil of Rye for Monongahela and Bourbon Whiskies		5 00
Essences		5 00

	Per gal.
Extract Holland and London Gin, 1 gallon for half a pipe	$ 5 00
Flavorings of every description.......	5 00
Neutralizing for age and body preparations, 1 gallon for 20 barrels........	10 00
Cherry and other juices from.........	$1 50 to 2 00

To this list is added the following recipe for making gin: "To 700 gallons of second quality rectified spirits add 70 pounds juniper berries, 70 pounds coriander seed, 3½ pounds of oil of almond cake, 1½ pounds of angelica root, 6 pounds of licorice root, and 8 pounds of sulphuric acid."

Essence of sloe juice is used by these adulterators to give a dryness and color to wines. Essence of black currants produces both body and richness of flavor so much esteemed in good port wine. A solution of tannin in spirits gives the requisite astringency and true sherry flavor to inferior wines. Palm oil dissolved in spirits imparts a rich golden color to sherry. The chemist can always find ingredients for "doctoring" our drinks as required. The adulteration of champagne is carried on to a greater extent than that of any other wine. A fair sample of champagne can be made from cider, maple sugar, or gooseberries.

The above facts are sufficient evidence of the extent of this most culpable practice. Scotch and Irish whiskies, which were formerly made pure by illicit stills scattered over the hills and bogs of Ireland and Scotland, are now simulated by adding creosote to corn whisky to give it the desired smoky flavor. In England what is called "Parliament whisky" is that which pays the Government tax. The lower grades of this liquor are strengthened by the addition of strychnine, which increases its quantity. The more fatal effects among those suffering from delirium tremens are attributable to this cause.

Malt liquors do not escape adulteration. Some of the articles used for this purpose are flag root, *cannabis indicus*, capsicum, paradise seed, beans, pulverized alum, quassia, sulphate of ammonia, sulphate of iron, *cocculus indicus*, etc., etc., in accordance with the result to be produced.

A story is told of George the Fourth of England, who was considered a connoisseur in wine. In the

The Adulteration of Liquors.

early days of his dissipation he had in his possession a small quantity of choice wines. The gentlemen of his suite, who shared his appreciation of good wine, finding he did not call for it, had exhausted it almost to the last bottle. Soon after, what was their horror to hear the royal command that it should be forthcoming at an entertainment to be given on the day following. In the greatest consternation they sought a noted wine-brewer in the city and explained their dilemma.

"Have you any of the wine left?" said the adept.

"A couple of bottles," rejoined the distressed party.

"Send one of them and I will see that you have the necessary quantity on hand in time, only tell me the very latest moment it can be received, for it must be drunk immediately."

He kept his word. The deception was perfect and no discovery of the fictitious potation was made.

We subjoin a simple test of the purity of claret wine: Make a solution of caustic potash and put a single drop in a glass of wine and if unadulterated it will not be affected. If it is colored with logwood, it will turn reddish purple; if with elderberries, dark purple; if mulberries were used, a lighter shade of purple; if beet root, a clear red; if Brazil wood, muddy red, and if litmus has been introduced, a pale shade of violet is the result.

CHAPTER VII.

COMPARATIVE EFFECTS OF FERMENTED AND SPIRITUOUS LIQUORS.

ALTHOUGH alcohol is chemically the same in brandy, whisky, wine and beer, yet the relative effects of these liquors on the human organism differ very widely. The alcohol in wine and beer, honestly made from grapes and barley, does not intoxicate in the same degree as an equal amount taken in brandy and whisky. The probable reason of this is that the weightier portions of the wine or beer modify the action of this spirit on the system. Just how this is done, we cannot explain; but that such is its effect, is a demonstrable fact.

Wine seems to excite the social and genial traits of character. Though it intoxicates, it seldom renders the person irritable or combative. It has been variously regarded by ancient and modern writers. Solomon warns us not to "look upon the wine when it is red, when it giveth color in the cup," assuring us that it is a "mocker, and whosoever is deceived thereby is not wise." Shakespeare makes the unhappy Cassio most eloquently discourse on this favorite beverage: "O thou invisible spirit of wine! If thou hast no name to be known by, let us call thee devil." Horace took a happier view of the subject and probably expressed the spirit of his age: "What does not wine incite to? It discloses secrets, compels ratification of our hopes, urges on the coward to fight, removes care from the troubled mind, teaches the arts. Whom have not flowing cups made eloquent? Whom have they not made free and happy under pinching poverty?"

Whether wine was ever entitled to such an extravagant panegyric, is not of very great importance; it simply goes to show the high estimate in which it was held in that early time.

Liebig says that, "as a restorative, as a means of refreshment when the powers of life are exhausted, of giving animation and energy when man has to struggle with days of sorrow, as a means of protection against transient, organic disturbance, wine is surpassed by no product of nature."

In the history of the social life of France, wine has the honor of being esteemed the source of much of the brilliancy and vivacity of this people, some writers going so far as to say that the patriotism, politeness, undaunted courage and exquisite sense of personal dignity characteristic of the French nation, are largely due to the general use of this favorite beverage. That such an aggregate of virtues can be justly attributed to wine, is an open question; but that it is more conducive to the growth of such qualities than the drinking of either beer or whisky, is undoubtedly true. For the mass of people in Great Britain and America, foreign wines are too expensive, and as a consequence a taste for spirituous liquors has been substituted among them.

Unlike the stimulation of wine and whisky, beer dulls and stupefies the brain. When it is adulterated or excessively fortified, its influence is similar to that of distilled liquors. Beer is not apt to render the individual belligerent or aggressive. Germans rarely quarrel over their glass, and are proverbially a peace-loving, law-abiding people. Their partiality for this drink is a recognized characteristic. When under its influence, they are eminently social and cheerful until the brain becomes overpowered by excessive imbibition, when they become not drunk, but *besotted*.

Brandy, whisky and other spirituous liquors, have a more immediate and direct effect on the nerves and brain than does either wine or beer. If taken in larger quantity than would serve merely to stimulate, they excite in an abnormal degree the most conspicuous traits in the person. As, for instance, the musical man sings, the piously inclined prays and exhorts, the sympathetic sheds tears, the orator becomes declamatory, the hilarious man boisterous, the pugilist combative, and so on through all the category of human idiosyncrasies. Viewed in this light, it would seem that the baser instincts are too often in the ascendency in man, when we take into consideration the fact that a majority of the crimes committed can be traced to the direct or indirect influence of ardent spirits.

We can only treat of the comparative effects of liquors in a general and not in a particular sense, as the individual differences of people must in a great measure determine the actual sequence of their use.

Enough facts, however, can be deduced from this general compilation to make it evident that fermented liquors are far preferable to spirituous ones. If we must drink such beverages, let them be wine or beer rather than whisky, brandy, etc. When we pass in review the long list of horrors attendant on intoxication, we are convinced that it would be a decided step in the right direction if appropriate legislation were made to encourage the consumption of fermented liquors, and decrease the consumption of spirituous ones.

CHAPTER VIII.

THE PHYSIOLOGICAL ACTION OF ALCOHOL.

WHEN taken into the stomach in the form of brandy, whisky or other distilled spirits, alcohol is not immediately absorbed but remains as an irritant to the mucous coating, until, by the process of exosmose and endosmose, transudation takes place between the spirit and the watery portion of the blood. When sufficiently diluted, it is taken up by the absorbents. If applied to the skin, a like process is carried on. If diluted before imbibing it does not irritate the stomach to the same extent, and absorption is more rapid. It then enters the general circulation through the veins and is conveyed to the heart through the right ventricle, from there to the right auricle, and thence to the lungs, where a portion is set free by expiration. The remainder returns immediately to the heart by the left ventricle, from there to the left auricle, and thence through the aorta to the brain and circulatory system, and again returns to the heart, making the circuit in about two and a half minutes. As the blood passes through every organ of the body, the tissues are either nourished or poisoned thereby. Thus health depends on the purity and integrity of the arterial blood. The effect of alcohol is evanescent unless frequent imbibitions follow each other, when the blood and tissues become saturated the brain unduly excited, and the individual exhibits in excess his most dominant trait of character. Finally he loses all control of his reasoning faculties, his locomotion becomes uncertain, and then altogether ceases; total paralysis supervenes, and we look with disgust upon the helpless mass of flesh reduced to that pitiable condition familiarly known as "dead drunk."

The habitual drunkard never dilutes his liquor; he invariably takes it "straight," as the saying is. This excess of stimulation produces a constantly increasing inflammation of the stomach which can only result in exhaustion of the vitality of that organ, when reaction follows with its attendant horror, *delirium tremens.*

Inebriates are divided into two distinct classes. The first is the man who drinks excessively for a short season and then resigns himself to the after effects, which are mild or severe according to the amount of liquor drunk and the strength of his constitution. After paying Nature's penalty for violating her laws, he observes a rigid abstinence for weeks or months as the case may be until his cravings again overpower him, and another "spree" is the invariable consequence. He may continue in this course for years, as Nature applies her healing balm to his outraged system during his interval of self-denial. The second class is largely in the majority. It includes all those who are rarely free from the influence of ardent spirits, but who do not become intoxicated to an extent that unfits them for daily attendance to their business. The amount of liquor drunk must increase with the continuance of the habit until it sometimes reaches the extent of more than a quart a day. In such persons, *delirium tremens* is always more severe and often proves fatal. As an illustration of the terrible suffering that a habitual drunkard endures while wrestling with this disease, I quote the following language of John B. Gough: "For three days I endured more agony than pen can describe, even though it were guided by a Dante. Who can relate the horrors of that frightful malady, aggravated as it is by the ever-present consciousness that it is self-sought. Hideous faces appeared on the walls and ceilings and on the floors; foul things crept along the bedclothes, and glaring eyes peered into mine. I was at one time surrounded by millions of monstrous spiders, which crawled slowly, slowly over every limb, whilst beaded drops of prespiration would start to my brow, and I would shiver until the bed trembled. Again, strange lights would dance before my eyes, and then suddenly the very blackness of darkness would appal me by its dense gloom. All at once while gazing at a frightful creation of my distempered mind, I seemed struck with sudden blindness. I knew a candle was burning in the room, but I could not see it. All was pitchy dark. I lost the sense of feeling, too, for I endeavored to grasp my arm in one hand, but consciousness was gone. I put my hand to my side, my head, but felt nothing; and still I knew my limbs and my frame were there. Then the scene would change; I was falling, falling swiftly as an arrow, far down in some terrible abyss; and so like reality was it that as I fell I could discern on the rocky sides of the precipitous shaft, mocking, gibing, fiend-like forms. I could feel the air rushing past me, making my hair stream out by the force of the unwholesome blast. The paroxysm would sometimes cease for a few moments, when I would sink back to my pillow drenched with perspiration, utterly exhausted, and feeling a dreadful certainty of the renewal of my torments."

Alcohol has two marked effects on the circulation. In the first place it quickens the action of the heart, which gives an additional force to the blood, and again it relaxes the blood-vessels on the surface of the body by influencing the nerves that contract and expand them. Hence the diffused glow that is experienced almost immediately after taking a glass of spirits. The flushing of the face, supposed to be due to an increase of temperature, is nothing more than the radiation from an enlarged surface of blood. As this enlarged quantity of blood is diffused over the surface of the body by the dilation of the vessels and increase of the circulation, a rapid cooling off by radiation is the result, and the chilled fluid is soon after carried back to the internal organs. Thus the common practice of taking a glass of spirits to keep *out* the cold, has the contrary effect of letting *in* the cold. This apparent increase of temperature, which is in reality a cooling process, renders the system less able to resist cold, especially in extreme cases.

The experience of such American and English navigators as Ross, Perry, Franklin and Kane, has demonstrated the pernicious effects of alcoholic liquors in the polar latitudes. The Russians have long been aware of this fact. Their soldiers are under orders not to drink anything of an intoxicating nature on the morning of a prospective march. To insure obedience to this command, it is the Corporal's duty to note the breath of every man in his regiment, when they are assembled after breakfast. Anyone found to have taken spirits is forthwith sent out of the ranks as being unfitted to withstand the frost and snow of a winter's march in that rigorous climate.

As a graphic illustration of the injurious results of spirituous drinks in extremely cold weather, we set down in full a narrative related by Mr. L. E. McKinley:—

"A group of twenty-six men, traveling over a Western plain, lost their way and were overtaken by darkness. The weather was severely cold and became more so as the night advanced. Though well provided with food, clothing, and plenty of whisky, they had no wood or fuel of any kind. The occurrences of the night are given in the language of the only physician who accompanied the exhibition. He was a man of good, strong, hard sense, with quite creditable medical attainments, considering the limited opportunities he had had, which consisted in reading works on medical practice. He had only heard of but had never seen a medical college.

"Addressing the men he said: 'As we can't get wood, boys, we must keep warm or at least alive through the powers of Madam *Vis Medicatrix Naturæ.*

She is all right in any weather if we don't clog her, and pucker her forces. If I have got any medical knowledge at all, I am going to use it to-night, and the first thing I begin with is this: I am as fond of whisky as any man dare to be, but by the gods, the man that gets drunk to-night to keep warm, won't see the daylight! When the great God of the universe made man, the boss work of the earth, he made all other things first, and the elements too—not to rule over him and kill him, but to hunker down to his wants. But, boys, whisky was scored out of that bill of fare. The *vis medicatrix naturæ* is the highest of all other things, and if she ain't splintered up by our own d———d folly, she will ride safely through the storm.

"We have got to keep stirring round, or huddled up in the straw of the wagons, as many of us as can cram together. Each one will keep the other warm. We must all eat as much as possible, but whisky ain't the thing. This is what I told them all; but very few minded me. I did not taste a drop, nor did two other men. We took off our boots and overcoats, and then got on the straw, and put our blankets over us, and our overcoats on the top of them. We were only cold but did not suffer or freeze. Three were very cold and we heard them yelling nearly all night. They suffered very much, but were not frozen. They took very little whisky, but they took several thin drinks in the run of the night. Seven other fellows, that drank a good deal, had their toes and fingers scorched, but they got over it in a few weeks. Six of the boys, who drank pretty strong, were badly frozen and never got over it; and four, that got very boozy, were frozen so badly that they died three or four weeks afterwards. Only three were stiff dead by daylight. They got dead drunk, and as they did not make a fuss, the other boys thought the whisky was keeping out the cold, so they drank the stronger. I tell you, sir, they all suffered just according as they took in the whisky; those that got drunk froze to death; those who drank less, but too much, died after a while; those that drank only moderately, will feel it as long as they live; and those who took only thin drinks, were well-nigh shut up. We three didn't drink any; the *vis medicatrix naturæ* brought us through. All were strong and vigorous men, in the very bloom of life.'"

It is a very general but erroneous opinion among workmen, that when they are called upon to perform excessive and long-continued labor, alcoholic liquor of some kind is an absolute necessity to enable them to execute it.

As an illustration of the falsity of this conception, we relate the following.—

The change of the Great Western Railroad from a six-foot gauge to the ordinary gauge, required the continuous labor of a large number of men. They literally worked night and day until it was completed, stopping only for meals and an hour or so of sleep. They were allowed beer when eating but at other times, it was prohibited, and a drink of the sweetened water from boiled oatmeal substituted in its place. One man in every twenty was kept busy preparing this wholesome beverage. The work was done much better, more cheerfully, and in a shorter time than if beer or spirits had been given.

There is no doubt, however, that in certain emergencies alcoholic liquors, acting so quickly, and being so transitory in their effects on the system, are often very beneficial.

CHAPTER IX.

ALCOHOL AS FOOD.

As this subject has long been a matter of discussion among scientists, and is still a mooted question, we propose to devote a chapter to its consideration.

Liebig says in support of the affirmative, that "the food action of alcohol must be ranked with that of fat, starch, and sugar, because the chemical basis of all is carbon."

Every aliment taken into the human stomach as food, must contain the chemical constituents of sugar, starch, fat or albuminous substances, whether derived from the vegetable or the animal kingdom. In the process of digestion it receives the gastric juice of the stomach, the bile from the gall-duct, and the pancreatic and other juices from the abdominal region. If deficient in any one of these secretions, the digestion is either wholly or partially imperfect, and we cannot be assured that the entire product, or any portion of it, will be converted into blood. What is not digested must be eliminated from the system by the excretory organs.

Now admitting that carbon is the basic principle of alcohol, and the before-named substances, fat, starch and sugar, it does not follow as a natural sequence that it is identical with them in all other particulars. The constituent elements of alcohol are carbon, oxygen and hydrogen. Not being in combination with any animal or vegetable matter, it contains no nitrogen, which is the basis of all tissue-forming foods.

Being wholly devoid of this essential element, it is impossible for it to undergo the process of digestion, which would fit it for assimilation by the different organs, and, consequently, cannot be considered an aliment. It is the height of absurdity to assert that it "must be ranked with fat, starch and sugar,', which are pre-eminently tissue-forming foods.

Another statement, equally erroneous, is made by Hargreaves in his work entitled "Alcohol and Science." He says: "Although alcohol is not a tissue-forming food, it is a calorific agent; and by its power of generating heat in the system, which is a necessity to digestion, it takes the place of food, and should be regarded as a respiratory and heat-producing aliment."

In a normal condition of the stomach, when food is introduced, it not only provokes the flow of the gastric juice, but it stimulates the evolving of a proper temperature necessary for digestion. Nature is very exacting in her demands; if the heat is above or below the proper degree, the digestion is retarded or prevented altogether. It is a knowledge of the exact temperature required in the process of fermentation that enables the wine manufacturer, and the brewer, to perfect their products.

Now alcohol by its presence in the stomach increases the heat above the requirements of the digestive apparatus, vitiates the gastric juice, and not being a solvent of food like the latter, or water, it impairs and impedes nature in her work. If by any possibility an increase of normal temperature in the stomach would be an aid to its work, then food would more easily digest when an excess of heat was generated by any morbific condition of the system, whereas, we know to the contrary.

It is affirmed that alcohol effects another serious injury to the stomach by vitiating the most important component of the gastric juice—pepsin. It precipitates and coagulates this ingredient, rendering it wholly or partially unable to disolve alimentary substances.

It is difficult, therefore, to perceive wherein alcohol can be justly considered by Mr. Hargreaves as "a respiratory and heat-producing food."

The same writer says farther on that "alcohol retards the destruction of tissue. By this destruction, force is generated, causing muscles to contract, organs to secrete and excrete. Now, as alcohol stops the full tide of this decay, it is very evident it must also furnish the force which is developed under its use. How it does this, is not clear.

"Although alcohol is not a tissue-forming food, yet it indirectly supplies the place of such, by retarding the metamorphosis of tissue, preventing the waste of muscle, and thereby preserving the strength and upholding the power of life."

This argument he handles discursively and ingeniously throughout the work, and from its promi-

ALCOHOL AS FOOD.

nence rather than its conclusive logic, it deserves more than a passing notice.

It is generally admitted that food does not furnish any force to the human system, until it has first been digested and converted into blood. In this form it is the vital nourishment of the tissues and organs, and is appropriated by every portion of the body by a process of assimilation, technically known as "Progressive Metamorphosis." It is well known that with every functional action of these organs of the body a certain amount of tissue is decomposed just as the production of steam is co-existent with the combustion of fuel. No force is ever created; it is simply produced by evolution or the setting free of another force. Every act, whether mental or physical, results in the destruction of tissue. Thought is evolved from the combustion of brain matter; the force to secrete gastric juice, from the combustion of some portion of the stomach, and the force that generates bile, from the consumption of certain substances of the liver, and so on through the entire organism. Thus from the destruction of one force, another is evolved. These postulates are axiomatic, and here comes in the operation of another law—the law of compensation—which in the order of nature is inexorable. If the production of one force from the destruction of another is not compensated for, an exhaustion or wasting of the material from which the force was evolved, follows. As in the instance of steam, the power generated by the burning fuel is not replaced; the steam does its work and escapes, and as a consequence its production is coincident with the consumption of fuel.

The same would be true of the body were it not for the continual formative processes going on from the digestion of food whereby new particles are deposited to take the place of the old. Were it not for this substitution of living atoms for decayed, death would soon result. In a perfectly healthy organism this interchange is co-equal. The cast-off tissue is taken up by the absorbents as effete matter and carried into the circulation, and is ultimately eliminated by the excretories.

All force is produced by the destruction of tissue, yet Mr. Hargreaves states that "alcohol, by retarding this destruction, must furnish the force which is developed under its use. How it does this," he further says, "is not very clear," and with this last acknowledgment we most heartily agree.

Alcohol stimulates the system beyond its natural condition, but it is at the expense of the latent vital forces. This expenditure cannot be compensated for, because this spirit, as we have proven, contains none of the elements of food. We admit that alcohol obstructs the metamorphosis of tissue by preventing the absorbents from taking it up. This effete matter, however, cannot be used over again, any more than ashes could be used to produce heat. It simply accumulates in the system, the body becomes loaded with impurities and does not lose flesh, which fact is used as an argument to prove the beneficial effect of alcohol in conserving tissue; but in reality, so far from "preserving the strength, and upholding the powers of life," the person is in a very unhealthy condition—the muscles become soft and spongy, the flesh bloated, and the general rectitude of the system is impaired. We beg, therefore, to differ with the learned scientists who claim that by some mysterious process alcohol furnishes force *per se.*

Food, and food only, can supply the necessary nourishment and temperature of the body for the preservation of life.

CHAPTER X.

ALCOHOL AS A MEDICINE AND A POISON.

To deny that the legitimate use of alcohol is a blessing, would be to impugn the wisdom of the Creator, who permits its existence. It is only its abuse that is injurious. That it can be beneficially employed as a medicine in certain physical conditions, all physicians will certify. Where an immediate effect is desired, it works to a charm. In sudden emergencies its rapid absorption, and its special action on the nervous system, are of great practical value. The liquors usually given in such cases are brandy or whisky; of the two, the former, if pure, is preferable.

In an abnormal state of the system the most marked benefit is attained when the spirit administered *does not affect the brain*, though it be given in large quantities. In such instances it is supposed to undergo some chemical change by the action of the vital forces, thus forming new substances, which, having no affinity for the brain, are appropriated by the organism as a remedial agent for its own preservation. We have personally witnessed such cases where large doses of brandy were repeated without any perceptible influence upon the cerebral organs.

On the other hand, if the brain is stimulated or narcotized by the brandy, this chemical change *cannot take place*, and the persistent use of the liquor would result seriously to the patient. In exhaustive diseases, and in sudden prostrations of the system, alcoholic stimulants are of great service in arousing the vital forces for a limited period until nature can react. Their continued use in any case is always injurious, and productive of fatal consequences in the long run.

Physicians make a grave mistake in teaching and inculcating the fallacy that alcohol imparts strength. The feeling of comfort and vigor that comes with its presence in the circulation is always transitory and must sooner or later be followed by a corresponding sensation of depression. Each reaction will be harder to overcome than the preceding one, for alcohol cannot increase functional powers, as it has nothing of nourishment to give to the system, as has been previously shown.

It may not be out of place here to devote a little attention to the consideration of the problem as to what becomes of alcohol when taken into the blood. This has long been a question of importance, both in medicine and organic chemistry. Some scientists contend that it is subject to no change while passing through the system, but is eliminated through the lungs, skin, and kidneys as alcohol still; that it is not oxidized in the lungs and expired as carbonic acid gas, but as alcohol, which is always detected in the breath. This is undoubtedly the natural effect of alcohol in a healthy state of the body.

Others affirm that in some diseased conditions it does undergo oxidation, or, if not that, some other chemical change takes place. The preponderance of evidence goes to prove that there are diseases wherein alcohol comes in contact with the morbid secretions in the circulation, when an interchange of elements takes place and new combinations are formed which act remedially on the system. This is the reason that large quantities of brandy, as before demonstrated, can be administered to some patients without special action on the brain. The specific nature of this chemical interchange of elements can never be known, as we cannot go behind a law of nature.

That alcohol is a poison few will doubt. If enough is taken it will destroy life in a short space of time. Its continued presence in the body will bring on various diseases of the heart, lungs, kidneys, and stomach. The most trivial causes render the inveterate drinker liable to affections of these organs, as the predisposing agent is always at work in his constitution. Fatty degeneration of the heart, kidneys, etc., and the "hob-nailed" liver, so called, are examples of the diseases directly attributable to ardent spirits. Thousands of wretched victims have been sacrificed annually to the excessive use of these deleterious substances. Lives that promised a rich autumnal fruitage have faded in their early spring or summer-time, leaving desolate hundreds of once happy homes.

Beer and porter, when habitually taken in large quantities, prevent the metamorphosis of tissue as before elaborated, and so clog the bodily machinery that the whole system becomes diseased. The retention of this effete nitrogen and carbon leads to an increase of bulk, dulls the brain, and the entire organism becomes lethargic.

The worst patients that enter the London hospitals are the brewer men. A bruise or scratch which in others would be insignificant, in them will often fester and mortify. Every medical man in London dreads a surgical operation on a patient who has been a confirmed beer drinker. In such cases the mortality is frightful. The habitual use of these beverages causes many of the serious diseases prevalent among people of advanced age.

We have no evidence that pure, light wines have any deleterious effects upon the human system when employed with reasonable moderation.

CHAPTER XI.

ALCOHOL AS A STIMULANT AND A NARCOTIC.

Few things in physiology are more important to understand than wherein lies the difference between a stimulant and a narcotic. The same substance can often be used to produce either effect, according to the quantity administered and the physical condition of the patient. The determining of the amount necessary to bring about a desired result, is a matter that can only be decided by a wise and experienced physician. The same dose at different times may vary in its effects, owing to a change in the state of the system.

In one form or another, the use of some kind of stimulant is almost universal among all nations, whether barbarous or civilized, and the secrets of nature have been invaded to concoct a variety of narcotic compounds. The Chinaman has his opium, the Hindoo his *hashish*, the European and American their alcohol and morphia, and millions of people in all climes are more or less addicted to the use of tea and coffee. No habit is so firmly fixed on mankind as that of stimulation. Its very universality would almost convince one that it is a natural, and, therefore, perfectly harmless practice; that a moderate use of stimulants but answers to an inborn instinct in the race, and its gratification is but an aid to progress

ALCOHOL AS A STIMULANT.

and happiness. We certainly know that it is no easy matter to deprive most people of their favorite drink, or drug, even though they may be partially or wholly aware of its injurious effects.

It is a question with physiologists whether the taking of unadulterated wine or beer at meals is not more wholesome than the drinking of tea and coffee. The latter custom is more prevalent in American families, while the former is an established habit in many European countries, and also in China and Japan.

Small doses of alcohol or opium give a feeling of relief and strength that passes off without any in-injurious reaction unless a repetition is resorted to. If taken in excess, the forces of nature are intensified, and if still greater quantities are used, the brain becomes narcotized. It will be seen, therefore, that small potions of alcohol or doses of morphia act as a stimulant to produce that exhilarating and elastic state so eagerly sought by the habitual partaker of either, while larger amounts of the same are admitted to be powerful narcotics. Their employment has been injuriously frequent and unnecessary among even our best physicians. Especially is this so of morphia, administered either hypodermically or otherwise, to quiet pain that is neither extreme nor unendurable. It generally gives immediate relief, but must usually be repeated, and it is doubtful if it has ever removed disease.

As long as the system is under the influence of a narcotic, no other medicine, if administered, can have its full effect, owing to the depression of the vital forces. For the same reason all pain and suffering, which are the indices of disease, are suppressed, and the physician finds it impossible to locate the malady, or form a correct judgment as to its cause or intensity. If the disease is not a serious one, as, for instance, an acute attack of neuralgia, the vitality will overcome both the disorder and the drug; but if the case is of a dangerous character, and the patient is persistently kept under its influence, death is almost sure to result, it being only a question of time.

The true province of the physician is to discover the cause of a disease and to assist Nature in removing it, always with a reverent conviction that, of the two, himself or Nature, she is invariably the wiser. It requires little medical knowledge to administer alcohol or morphia, but a proper understanding of the laws that govern our being is a profounder matter, and one of far deeper moment to ourselves and humanity.

So popular has this practice of narcotizing become in the medical profession that it is time that strenuous efforts were made to convince people that its use is dangerous. In this age of progressive thought, we ought to know that anything that paralyzes the efforts of nature when she is working to her utmost to cast out disease, is wholly unreasonable, and, alas! too often fatal in its results.

This prescribing of narcotics has led thousands of men and women to become confirmed in the use of morphia, from whose relentless grasp escape is almost impossible.

CHAPTER XII.

LICENSING SYSTEMS OF GREAT BRITAIN AND AMERICA.

The granting of licenses for the sale of spirituous liquors is not of recent origin. It dates back in England some hundreds of years. Such licenses were first granted by justices of the peace, and security required of the applicant for good conduct and proper management of the house. This right was exercised by these officers of the law for nearly three hundred years.

During the early part of the present century this law was changed and the exclusive authority to grant licenses for the sale of alcoholic beverages was transferred to the Commissioners of Excise on the payment of a certain sum, and the presentation of a certificate of character signed by six rate-payers. The natural result of these easy terms was a rapid increase of saloons, for the poorest and lowest characters were able to obtain the right to maintain them. Two classes of licenses were granted: One permitting liquor to be drunk on the premises, and one to be drunk off the premises. The latter was seldom required and consequently the country was overrun with small drinking houses.

In 1869 Parliament passed an act assigning to the magistracy the right of giving certificates, which alone should entitle the grantees to obtain licenses for the sale of malt liquors. The magistrates of small towns and rural districts receive no salary, and are generally chosen from the most wealthy and influential class in the township. Owing to the great patronage they possessed, and having the exclusive privilege of granting licenses, many designing and unscrupulous persons secured appointments. As a consequence, monopolies were created by them to establish, control and prevent competition, and so corrupt did this system of licensing become, that a strong desire for some kind of reformation was engendered in the minds of the people. Their efforts to bring about a change were strenuously opposed by the powerful body of liquor manufacturers and dealers.

The House of Lords appointed a select committee, in 1877, to investigate the subjoined practical questions bearing on the subject:—

"*First*—Has past legislation been effective in diminishing the amount of drunkenness which unfortunately prevails in the most populous districts of the country?

"*Second*—Are we likely to effect this object either by amending the provisions of the laws now in force, or by introducing some entire new system of licensing?"

The report of the committee on these questions was substantially as follows: To the first proposition they gave a distinctively negative answer; and to the second they recommended that legal facilities be given to municipalities for adopting either Mr. Chamberlain's plan or the "Gothenburg system," neither of which they positively indorsed.

Up to the appointment of this committee, two classes of licenses, as before said, were granted by Justices of the Peace, to sell excisable liquors by retail: One class to be drunk on the premises and the other to be drunk off the premises. The former were issued under magisterial discretion; the latter he had not the power of refusal. These were granted under the system of free trade, which after experience proved to be a failure, they not being sufficiently remunerative, because like privileges were contained in those issued by magisterial discretion. The committee recommended some change of doubtful importance for the amendment of the licensing laws, with little hope that any legislative enactment could materially diminish the consumption of spirituous liquors. They proposed the following bill:—

"That on Sundays licensed houses in the metropolis should be open from 1 to 3 P. M. for consumption *off* the premises, and from 7 to 11 P. M. for consumption *on* the premises. That in other places in England they should be open from 12:30 to 2:30 P. M. for drinking *off* the premises, and for consumption *on* the premises from 7 to 10 P. M., in popular places, and from 7 to 9 P. M. in other places." This bill was rejected.

On the 15th of November, 1876, at a meeting of the "Birmingham Liberal Association" in England, the annexed resolution, presented by Mr. Chamberlain, was adopted:—

"That in the opinion of this meeting it is desirable that local representative authorities should be empowered to acquire, on payment of fair compensation, on a principle to be fixed by Parliament, all existing interests in the retail sale of intoxicating drinks, within their respective districts, and thereafter, if they see fit to carry on the trade for the convenience and on behalf of the inhabitants, but so that no individual shall have any pecuniary interest in, or derive any profit from, such sale."

The adoption of this resolution called out a speech from Mr. Chamberlain, in which he proposed a plan for the suppression of intemperance; it ran as follows: "Town councils might be empowered, after giving the usual notice, and on payment of fair compensation, based on the average profits of the last three years, to acquire any or all of the licenses within its jurisdiction. At the same time the powers possessed by the licensing justices and committees might be vested in the councils, only with an appeal to the high court of justice, and subject to the provision that no new license should be granted until the proportion had been reduced to, say, one in five hundred of the population.

"Power should be given to the councils to deal with all, or any, of the houses acquired by them, in any of the following ways, namely: (a) To abandon them altogether; (b) to grant licenses to the highest bidder under conditions to be fixed by the council, and for a period not exceeding five years; (c) to carry on the trade in the present premises, rented or purchased for the purpose, under the conduct of managers, with remuneration independent of the amount of, or profit on, the sale of intoxicating drinks.

"In the last two cases the amount received from the sale of licenses, or as profit from the traffic, should be carried to a license fund, to be applied as follows: (1) To pay interest on all loans contracted for purchase of license on premises; (2) to create a sinking fund to extinguish loans in twenty years from date; (3) to pay all costs of management and expenses of carrying out the act; (4) to buy up and extinguish licenses till the maximum proportion of one to five hundred of the population has been reached; (5) the surplus, if any, to be used, first, in securing the earlier repayment of the loans contracted till these are wholly liquidated, and then the balance to be carried to the credit of the education-rate, and poor-rate, in fixed proportions."

These were the views of Mr. Chamberlain at that time. Afterwards he modified them in various particulars. He relinquished the plan of compensating the publicans on the profits of the last three years, discarding the idea of granting licenses to anyone, and leaving the entire matter to Parliament. Instead of buying up a part of the public drinking houses he proposed to buy them all; and in the place of a fixed principle of valuation, he insisted that the town should be ready to pay whatever Parliament may choose to decide.

The forcible suppression of a trade, made lawful by the possession of licenses from competent authorities, would establish a principle on which Parliament dare not venture; consequently Mr. Chamberlain's plan was not carried into effect. To do so would have given an immense influence to the town council, who are too often the paid subjects of the liquor ring. Such monopolies are dangerous to individual and political interests. Any law that is founded on taking forcibly from a man his legitimate means of livelihood, no matter how disreputable it appears in the eyes of the community, is an unjust one and does not deserve the support of the people. The privilege he enjoys was granted him by the constituted authorities, for which he paid the sum they demanded of him; and to deprive him of the right to maintain a business made lawful by such legal enactments, is a violation of every principle of equity, and could not fail to be disastrous in its effects, and do no good whatever in reforming the drinking habits of the community.

The other system of licensing recommended by the committee appointed by the House of Lords, was one that had its origin in Gothenburg, Sweden. Some wealthy citizens of that city formed a company for controlling the sale of liquor in their district. They purchased enough for the demand of the town and allowed none but their own employes, or parties authorized by the association, to sell it out to the people. All intoxicating liquors had to be procured from the company, and no person was allowed to profit by the sale, except as it indirectly increased his trade in other goods.

The larger cities of Sweden did not adopt the

Gothenburg plan. A monopoly of any kind is not usually relished by the masses. A law that is not of permanent benefit or of universal application, will not command the support of the people at large.

Another method of licensing worthy of notice is one that is practiced in Brattleboro, England. A detail of a particular case will show the practical workings of the plan:—

A is intoxicated, and because of such intoxication becomes a disturber of the peace. He is arrested and sent to the lock-up, and when sober is brought before a magistrate and fined $5.00 and costs. In default of payment he is committed to the county jail, where he remains until the fine is paid. In his examination he is compelled under the law to disclose where he obtained his liquor (the law is imperative on this point). The liquor-seller is then arrested, and if the offense is proved, he is fined $10 and costs, and, if the case is aggravated, a larger fine is affixed.

This law was practically in the hands of the bailiffs of the villages, or the common council of larger towns. Another of its features was the closing of all saloons on Sundays.

In other places than Brattleboro the enforcement of this law has been attended with only partial success. Every form of deception and perjury was resorted to by the people to defeat its establishment, thus developing a condition of morals that could hardly be worse than intemperance itself.

France, Italy, Spain, Hungary and Germany have no restrictive laws as regards intoxicating drinks, and still there is very little immoderate drinking in these countries; while our statute books and those of Great Britain are filled with prohibitory laws, and yet intemperance is a national vice.

To raise a revenue by the sale of that which debases the people, is not only a prolific source of crime and pauperism, but the cost to the country, annually, is many times more than the sums received therefrom. Therefore it will be seen that from a pecuniary point of view, even, the policy of these laws is doubtful.

As regards high and low license, the basis of the two is the same, the only difference being that high license decreases the number of saloons; but, it is a practical illustration of the vicious principle of one law for the rich, and another for the poor.

No valid objection can be raised against the licensing system *per se* as a means of raising the necessary governmental revenue; but there is just cause for censure when discriminations are made. There should be an equal taxation on every business in proportion to the amount of capital employed and the income derived therefrom. Such uniform licensing would render every occupation legitimate in the eyes of the law. It is no extenuation to say that the business for which the higher license is charged, is not considered equally reputable. If this is really the case, a license should not have been granted, but if granted, this act of the authorities renders the business, by law, thoroughly respectable, and they have no right to go back of their own action. Their discrimination against saloons, therefore, is unjust and not in accordance with the spirit of the law.

Admitting that saloons are, as a rule, disreputable, and saloon-keepers notoriously bad citizens, yet they have a right to equal privilege and protection under a law that has licensed their business.

After a careful examination of the subject, we are forced to acknowledge that no method of licensing so far employed, has been a successful means of overcoming the evil of intemperance. We must look to other ways for its accomplishment.

CHAPTER XIII.

AMERICAN LIQUOR LAWS.

Long before the temperance movement was afoot, English and American statesmen thought it an absolute necessity to place legal restraint on the liquor traffic, and so inaugurated special license systems, to meet the exigencies of the case. This arrangement undoubtedly led to fewer numbers of dealers, for previously the profits of the business were so great, and the amount of capital and skill required so little, that there was a constant pressure into it of the indolent, shiftless and vicious; but it also lent moral support to the traffic by giving it the sanction of law It may well be asked if society, as a corporate body, is justified in legalizing the office of tempter in placing before the weak and untrained, temptations to which they in their *present moral* condition, must inevitably succumb; then afterwards adding to the misery of such unfortunates a penalty, while at the same time upholding by law the cause of their degradation.

For more than forty years a persistent and energetic agitation has been maintained in the more populous States of the Union on the liquor problem. There is hardly a remedy suggested by the mind of man that has not been used to stay the growing evil of intemperance.

It may not be generally known that the Federal Government asserts the right to grant licenses through its own officers for the sale of spirituous liquors in every State in the Union. The United States Commissioners will grant a license to any citizen in the State, on the payment of $25, to sell spirituous liquors in their original packages as imported, which cannot be seized by the State authorities.

It will be readily seen that this law must, from its very nature, thwart in a great measure the success of any local or State prohibitory law.

Maine has been the leading State in the prohibition movement. The following is a synopsis of the laws adopted in her Legislature in 1851:—

FIRST SECTION

Prohibits the manufacture or sale of intoxicating liquor except as is hereinafter provided.

SECOND SECTION

Authorizes Select Men, Mayor and Aldermen, to appoint an agent to sell intoxicating liquor for medicinal and manufacturing purposes and no other.

THIRD SECTION

Gives bonds for faithful performance.

FOURTH SECTION

Describes penalties for violation.

FIFTH SECTION

Prescribes the mode of applying the law to offenders.

SIXTH SECTION

Treats of appeal.

SEVENTH SECTION

Treats of agents who perfect their bonds.

EIGHTH SECTION

Treats of makers and common sellers.

NINTH SECTION

Excludes persons engaged in unlawful traffic in intoxicating liquors from juries and cases arising under this act.

TENTH SECTION

Gives precedence in court over all other business on appeal.

ELEVENTH SECTION

Authorizes a Justice of the Peace or any Municipal or Police Judge to grant a warrant of search to any Sheriff, City Marshal, or any constable who shall proceed to search the premises described in said warrant on the affidavit of three reputable persons. If any spirituous or intoxicating liquors be found, such liquors are forfeited to the State.

The other sections describe the mode and manner of proceedings on appeal, convictions, forfeitures and penalties.

So completely does the list cover the entire question that escape by the quirks and subtleties of law is almost an impossibility. The punishment of the first offense is $10 fine; of the second, $20 fine and costs; of the third offense, $20 fine and costs, and in addition, imprisonment of from three to six months.

This law was tried and subsequently abandoned

in Massachusetts, Rhode Island and Connecticut. It still remains in the statutes of New Hamphire, but is not enforced. In Vermont it is as stringently carried out as in Maine. Similar laws have been enacted with more or less success in Iowa, Kansas and several other States.

Massachusetts has recently passed a law under provision of which licenses of five different classes are granted:—

First, To sell liquors of any kind to be drunk *on* the premises.

Second, To sell malt liquors, cider, and light wines to be drunk *on* the premises.

Third, To sell malt liquors and cider, to be drunk *on* the premises.

Fourth, To sell liquors of any kind *not* to be drunk on the premises.

Fifth, To sell malt liquors, cider and light wines *not* to be drunk on the premises.

The penalties for selling to minors and for any injury done by an intoxicated person, or loss sustained on account of such intoxication, are similar to those of the State of Ohio. In the latter State and in Michigan, there are clauses in their constitutions, forbidding the granting of licenses "to sell in any quantity intoxicating liquors to be drunk in, upon, or about the building or premises, or to sell such intoxicating liquor to be drunk in any adjoining room, building, or premises, or other place of public resort connected with such building."

Places where intoxicating liquors are sold in violation of this act, are declared nuisances, and power is given to the authorities to close them.

The seller of such liquors to minors, or to any intoxicated person, or to those who are in the habit of drinking to excess, is subject to a fine and imprisonment, and to damages which the wife, child, parent, guardian, or other party who shall be injured in person, or property, or means of support in consequence, can lawfully collect.

The prohibitory laws of Michigan are more effective than those of any other State in the Union. When appeal is taken to her Superior Court, the accused has to file bonds in the sum of two thousand dollars, with not less than two good and sufficient sureties, conditioned that during the pending of the suit he will not sell intoxicating drinks.

In considering local option from a superficial standpoint, it seems perfectly right that a majority in any town or district should be justified in deciding whether spirituous liquors should or should not be sold in their particular locality.

This subject, however, does not come within the province of law or politics; it is one of individual rights. In a question of law, the people have the privilege of duly electing their chosen men for the Legislature and of sending their representatives to Congress to decide by a majority vote if such and such a law shall be passed. Laws are not made to prevent a man from doing either right or wrong. He is always at liberty to do what he pleases, but if his act violates a law, he must suffer the penalty which the law inflicts for such violation.

In politics, also, the people have the right to decide by vote which party shall hold the reins of government in towns, cities, State and nation; but the question of drinking liquor is a personal one, and cannot be regarded as a crime, *per se*. For a majority, then, in any community to deny the minority the right to do what is not a crime, would be interfering with individual rights. Such interference is always despotic and not to be tolerated by a free government. The establishment of local option under prohibitory laws can only be considered as a far greater evil than that of intemperance, for it attacks the fundamental and most vital principle of civil liberty.

A bill on this question was submitted to the Parliament of Great Britain a few years ago by the "United Kingdom Alliance for the Reform of the License Laws," which reads as follows: "That inasmuch as the ancient and avowed object of licensing the sale of intoxicating liquors is to supply a supposed public want, without detriment to the public welfare, the House is of opinion that a legal power of restraining the issue or renewal of licenses should be placed in the hands of persons most deeply interested and affected, namely, the inhabitants themselves, who are entitled to protection from the injurious consequences of the present system, by some effective measure of local option."

Two hundred and fifty-two of the members voted against the bill, and one hundred and sixty-four for it. The objections urged against it were, first: that it would not be just to make a general law to prevent the innocent use of an article because some had abused it; second: that it would be less just to intrust such power to a local majority; third: that this same power to choose between enforcing or withdrawing this prohibition, would not be a practical remedy for intemperance."

It is difficult to see wherein it would be more just for a majority to dictate to the people what they should drink, than to say what they should eat, or to prevent the minority from procuring that which they may consider necessary to their health and happiness, so long as they respect the rights of others.

CHAPTER XIV.

SUMPTUARY LAWS.

EFFORTS are being continually made by various clergymen and members of churches to compel the Legislatures of different States to pass laws to prevent what they regard as the desecration of the Sabbath.

It is not in our province to discuss polemics any farther than to comprehend in what religionists elect to deprive the people. Has the term "desecration" any specific meaning alike interpreted by all classes, or is it variously understood?

In discussing this question we are confronted at the outset with the undoubted fact that what one conscientious person esteems a wrong, may be regarded as perfectly right and justifiable by another equally honest.

Religious people, as a rule, believe that attending church is an important external evidence of their moral status that must be observed, no matter at what cost or deprivation. They set their disapproving seal on the indulgence of all recreations or amusements of any kind on the Sabbath day, hoping to resist the tide of unbelief, and to be an aid to the temperance cause.

In Philadelphia, in 1860, through the influence of these Sabbatarians, the Crystal Palace, Zoological Gardens, libraries, picture galleries and all other places of amusement, were closed under the mistaken idea that people would consequently flock into the churches. On the contrary, a lower order of recreation was patronized, the saloons and beer-halls became overcrowded; the masses must have amusement and were not particular where they went to get it.

A much better plan would be to encourage all innocent diversions, especially cheap excursion trains to the open country. California is particularly favored in her suburban retreats for the toil-worn city laborer and his wife and children. Our elegantly fitted cable-cars furnish an unrivaled mode of transit to our parks, beaches and numerous picnic grounds, where Nature, in this climate, is ever prodigal in her gifts. In a recent sermon by Dr. Harcourt, of San Francisco, we find the following excellent remarks on the subject of amusements:—

"Many of us have drawn our somber ideas of religion from paganism. We have somehow formed the idea that black is the color most pleasing to heaven. Most of us have lingering around us the idea that a good laugh is not heavenly, and therefore ought to be suppressed. Away with such nonsense. We may be very happy and not irreligious, and we may be very solemn and not a bit religious. In man's nature there is a demand for amusement and recreation, and the church of the future cannot afford to overlook this fact nor fail to meet it. I believe in a healthy Christianity, a Christianity with sunshine in it. We have had enough of the sixteenth century sort. I only know of it from history and the traces of it yet lingering around some creeds, but the more I know of it the less I think of my ancestors. I do not want the church of the nineteenth century to drift back to the moldiness and the stupidity of the Dark Ages. I believe in all natural and healthful amusements. The more the better when under proper restraints. The great danger of the American people is not overplay but overwork. We have little time for anything else in our pursuit after the almighty dollar."

Dr. Harcourt further stated that he steadfastly believed that the theater might be made to serve as noble an end as the pulpit, but that it ever would, he seriously doubted.

At the best, the working classes can have but one day out of the seven to spend in such health-giving recreations, and the week's work afterwards will be more cheerfully resumed. A ride or walk through a flower-fringed park or along a glorious sea-beach is often an inducement to people to forego a less innocent pleasure, and, therefore, should be esteemed an aid to morality and a legitimate right to city residents. This privilege to the poor is of inestimable value, and should not be underrated by the wealthier class, who may enjoy themselves as they please during the week, and can, therefore, be better contented to remain housed up in church on Sundays. Viewed in this light it is not an easy matter to convince working people that the Sabbath should not be rightfully regarded a day of rest and recreation rather than of austere observances. Many of them are Germans, or of German extraction, and have been carefully trained in these habits. They are notedly fond of music and the drama, and are never so happy as when enjoying both, surrounded by their entire family, and it is a beautiful trait in his character that such a pleasure would be incomplete to him without his *"frau"* and *"kinder."* Any law abridging their Sunday liberties must, therefore, be especially obnoxious to them, and they comprise a large portion of our most desirable population. That their social habits are not particularly derogatory to morals the German character demonstrates. They are an honest, industrious, home-loving people, who seldom find their way to our almshouses or jails.

Coming to our country with habits and customs already formed, Germans naturally prefer mutual association where they can introduce among themselves the peculiar enjoyments to which they have been accustomed for generations past. As all these simple recreations are peaceable and law-abiding, it is unjust to legislate them out of existence. It is interfering with the divine prerogative of man and is both arbitrary and unconstitutional. No one has a right to dictate to another how he shall spend his Sundays so long as his habits do not infringe on those of his neighbor. Such dictation will not be endured by any class of American citizens, and only tends to create antagonism between the two extremes of society. The pages of history are darkened with the wrongs committed on the people by the enforcement of sumptuary laws established by clerical power. Now, however, the scepter has been wrested from their grasp, and is delegated to the public press, who hold omnipotent sway.

In the earnest efforts of the temperance advocates to abolish saloons, etc., they must not omit the establishment of reading-rooms, concert-halls, lunch-parlors, in fact, any home-like place where rest and innocent amusement can be had as cheap as the vicious pastimes furnished in the saloons and low dives. The latter are crowded by the ruder elements of society and are among the greatest evils in our large cities. They are usually underground, and here a low order of theatrical performance, with villainous music and bad whisky and beer are furnished to frequenters at cheap rates. A law prohibiting the keeping of such places would simply pave the road for the creation of like amusements in some other way equally objectionable. The class that visit these dives would be out of their element in more refined surroundings. It would be just as reasonable to expect a Digger Indian to appreciate the rapturous chords of Beethoven or the enchanting notes of Jenny Lind, as for one of these people. They have been born and reared in circumstances of poverty, vice and wretchedness. Their moral faculties are in abeyance to their habits of drinking, carousing and passional indulgences.

All progress and cultivation must be made by slow degrees. A child cannot be advanced from simple arithmetic to the higher branches of mathematics at a single step. Time works marvelous changes, but does it by gradual processes. One great reformation that could be made in these dives would be the prevention of the sale of spirituous liquors therein. Whisky is most frequently the cause of disturbances, and only wine and beer, and these unadulterated, should be sold to the *habitues*.

A proper conception of these Pariahs of the body politic ought to suggest that barbarous tribes alone do not need our missionaries, for the most debased of God's creatures are often our immediate neighbors.

A few years ago, in this State, the passing of laws to close up all places of public resort on Sundays was made an issue at the polls. It was voted down, and the zealous advocates of this step have never made a similar attempt.

An ancient authority has wisely said, "The Sabbath was made for man, not man for the Sabbath."

CHAPTER XV.

PROHIBITION.

The fearful results of intemperance are so sadly true that the welfare of every household in the land may be considered involved in the settlement of this question. There is an almost unanimous sentiment among all classes that this state of things should not go on; that some kind of restriction must be placed on the sale of intoxicating drinks. No one will deny that their excessive use is an unmixed evil, a vice without a single redeeming feature. Thus far a reasoning mind is on the side of the prohibitionist; but when he passes beyond the ground of pure ethics into that of practical, every-day life, another element is introduced into the question, and men seek to know what success prohibitory laws have already had. They naturally look to Maine, as she has had more than thirty years' experience in suppressing the liquor traffic. In these efforts she has been systematically upheld by her Legislature. Civil and penal statutes have been enacted and enforced, as thoroughly as was possible by human agencies, and yet Maine cannot be regarded as remarkable for sobriety. That the people drink less than they did, may be true; but this is equally true of the whole United States. In this respect it is admitted that there has been a material change in the habits of the people, and Maine has been no exception.

It is no easy matter to obtain statistics as to the amount of liquor consumed in a State where its sale and use are looked upon as a crime; but enough is known to furnish proof positive that if prohibitionists seek to build their cause on the successful operation of the law in Maine, they will find but a weak support in her history of the past third of a century.

Michigan has the most efficient of all the prohibitory laws, and yet they cannot be enforced in any of the cities, or larger towns and villages. In the more populous portions of the State it has become a dead letter.

Owing to the large proportion of foreign-born citizens in Iowa, the prohibitory laws of that State are not in successful operation.

The Governor of Rhode Island, in his message to the State Legislature, declares that "prohibitory laws are sadly inefficient for want of a proper public sentiment to support them. The attempt to enforce prohibition is a thankless undertaking, for, though it may represent public opinion, yet the carrying out of a law is almost wholly dependent upon the public will, as contra-distinguished from the public opinion. Without a will, the way cannot be found."

The above message is an expression of the common experience in every State that has prohibitory laws.

A writer in the Philadelphia *Review* says:—

"In Portland, Maine, and in Portsmouth, New Hampshire, I have seen more drunkards, in proportion to the population, than I ever saw in Philadelphia, where there are 1,500 saloons too many.

No matter how the liquor business is prohibited, liquor will be sold as long as there is a profit in the business. Old drunkards will have their dram, *no matter what it costs.* Neal Dow has fought the liquor interests here for thirty years or more, and yet there is as much sold and drunk here to-day as in other cities of its size in the country. An American citizen is an independent being. If you say he shall not, he will, in spite of all law, restrictions, etc., to the contrary notwithstanding. I have been a personal observer of prohibition in Maine, New Hampshire, Kansas, and towns in Colorado, and must confess that it is a farce that often does more harm than good. There is not a practical man in the nation but to-day is convinced that prohibition is a failure."

As an evidence of the many subterfuges and excuses resorted to in order to secure liquor, we insert the following somewhat humorous account taken from a Kansas paper:—

"Whisky sold in drug-stores, that are gin-mills on the sly, is not usually very good stuff. Your old drinker has no faith in the cocktail cure of the apothecary shop. In one Kansas county, where the prohibition law is in force, 2,812 sales of liquor for one month are recorded in the drug-stores; an amount of nine cases, 788 quarts, and 2,154 bottles. Almost every man pretended that something was the matter with him. Lager beer was the most popular medicine. Of all the ailments affected, indigestion was the most common. It appeared to be epidemic throughout the county. After it came biliousness, and whisky was claimed to be its only antidote. Heavy colds, also, accumulated, and there was much general debility, and a fearful lot of ague. One could be sure that it was the latter by the way the old hands shook.

"What we most admire about these Kansas people is their wonderful ingenuity in devising complaints that required the immediate application of some spirituous mixture. One man wished whisky to bathe his wife; another needed it for his horse's shoulder; a humane individual desired it for his cow, which had some peculiar disorder, and his friend thought his colt was similarly afflicted; while a third man wished to try it on a favorite mule. In fact, during a single week more than a dozen horses required whisky or brandy, three men had a touch of sun-stroke, and one more feared he had been bitten by a mad dog, while the calls from women for brandy and wine for mince pies and puddings were an every-day occurrence."

That prohibitory laws have disappointed the sanguine hopes of their honest advocates, and done little to reduce the number of drunkards, few can question. No one doubts the zeal and indefatigable energy of the noble men and women who have brought about this movement, and wherever they have lessened the number of saloons, and thus been the means of removing temptation from the people, they deserve the thanks and "Godspeed" of every true heart in the nation. If they have in a great measure failed in their cherished object, they have worked from a good motive.

PROHIBITION.

We insert the following excerpts taken from articles published in the New York *Nation* several years ago, which give some very excellent reasons why prohibition cannot be successfully carried out:—

"Such a law, if enforced, would be disobeyed and evaded to an extraordinary degree, even by people of reputable character. It is a matter of history that the drinking habits of society are as old as the race itself, and to attempt their eradication by special legislation, is an absolutely hopeless undertaking.

"The instincts of personal freedom are so indelibly instilled into the American mind that prohibitory laws are naturally more objectionable to them than they could possibly be to any other people. Any police interference with their customs is odious and offensive, and cannot fail to engender a spirit of opposition.

"The taking of some kind of stimulating drink is associated with the most important events in the lives of a great many. On occasions of births, marriages, and happy meetings of friends, the social glass together has been esteemed for ages the most effective mode of expressing feeling. There is nothing in the history of human nature to warrant the conclusion that it will ever be possible to prohibit acts by law which in themselves are considered harmless, because based on the fact that excess in the commission of them is hurtful. We all should set a good example, but whether we are called upon to refrain from doing that which is not wrong in itself, for the sake of preventing others from over-indulgence, is a question that must be left to each individual to decide for himself. It is argued that alcohol is a poison, and therefore its use should be prohibited. So are quinine, morphia, and most other drugs, when taken in excess, yet no one would expect their use to be prohibited by law.

"To strive to promote the interests of what is conceived to be a good cause, is highly commendable; but the intolerant spirit with which the disciples of total abstinence too often seek to enforce their doctrines and practices upon other members of society, is very reprehensible."

All human laws, to be of benefit to the people, must be based upon the divine law of right and justice. The founders of the Constitution of the United States aimed to have this law as its governing principle. Liberty of thought and action is insured to every man thereby, so long as he does not trespass on the rights of others.

All laws, State or federal, must be in accord with the Constitution of the United States, and no State has the right to pass any law which conflicts with it. A law, to be just and reasonable, must be capable of universal and impartial administration. These postulates we think will not be disputed.

The question now arises, Will laws for the prohibition of the manufacture and sale of intoxicating liquors stand these tests? Maine, and some other States, have passed laws prohibiting within their boundaries the manufacture, sale, and importation of spirituous liquors, either wholly or under onerous restrictions. As a consequence, distilleries and breweries have been closed, and this, too, without compensating their owners. Can such laws be equally felt by these men and the rest of the community? They were engaged in a business made legal by the laws of the United States, for neither of these industries is prohibited thereby.

There are not less than one million of the population of this country that are lawfully employed in making and selling intoxicants. In those States where distilleries and breweries are allowed to carry on their trade, every gallon of beer or spirits manufactured is taxed by the Federal Government, yielding in the aggregate an enormous revenue. It is not to be supposed that the United States is thus legalizing, and profiting by, what should be regarded as an unlawful calling. Therefore, no State has a right to close up industries that are made lawful by the laws of the United States, thus rendering valueless property that can only be used in the business for which it was intended. Such laws on the part of the State are arbitrary, tyrannical, and unconstitutional. These establishments supply a want in the community which, from the immense consumption of their products, must rather be considered a necessity than an article of luxury, as prohibitionists contend when urging their extinction.

People who do not feel disposed to forego the use of these beverages are compelled to provide themselves clandestinely by evasive means. This patronizing of other States for what should be manufactured in their own, not only increases the cost of liquor, but also encourages the crime of smuggling—if in this case it should be esteemed such. No law, however stringent, can deter a man in this country from obtaining what he wants if he has the money to pay for it.

The closing up of these industries is a pecuniary loss to the State as well as to the individual, as it prevents both foreign and interstate commerce, the investment of capital, and lessens taxation, thus directly and indirectly injuring local trade, and in various ways acting as an irritant to the people.

Some prohibition States have not closed their distilleries and breweries, but have allowed them to be carried on under certain restrictions. They are permitted to manufacture, but only for medicinal and manufacturing purposes, and for exportation to other States. This disregard for the moral welfare of their neighbors, while protecting their own State from demoralizing influences, is hardly in accordance with the principle, "Love your neighbor as yourself." Then again those States where prohibitory laws are not in force enjoy more or less monopoly in these industries, which has the effect of increasing their own wealth at the expense of the others.

Total prohibition is absolutely impossible under the existing laws of the United States, which legalizes the manufacture of intoxicants, and grants licenses for the sale of spirituous and other liquors in original packages in any State in the Union upon payment of a specified sum.

In preceding pages we have given a synopsis of

the prohibitory laws of different States, all of which have a like basis, and need not, therefore, be discussed *seriatim* under this heading. The principle involved in each of them is that of coercion. It was this principle which instigated the religious intolerance of the so-called Dark Ages, where for more than a thousand years unsuccessful efforts were made by cruel and tyrannical laws, to force people into one groove of religious thought.

It is to be hoped that in this more enlightened age we shall not be equally slow in making the discovery that coercive laws will not compel a people to adopt a universal belief, whether it be in total abstinence, religion or politics. It is the application of this element of force to crush out free thought and free action that has done much to retard the growth and progress of knowledge and civilization in the past centuries. Man can only advance in both when he is in the enjoyment of physical and mental freedom. He must have his choice from the good and evil fruits spread before him, and his reward or punishment is naturally evolved from the selection he makes. The effect of an act is always the direct consequence of the existing cause.

Moral suasion cannot make a favorable impression on the mind while repressive laws are in force, especially when they trammel the personal liberty guaranteed to every citizen by our Government. A man naturally says, "This is tyranny, and I will not submit to it." Even if the advice given is good, and suggests what he voluntarily would have done if left to himself, the attempt to compel him arouses a spirit of combativeness which is more or less inherent in every individual. Indeed, there is no attribute of the human mind more firmly engrafted and more easily aroused than this determined opposition to force.

What is the result of the attempt to enforce prohibitory laws upon the drinking classes? It arouses such a spirit of indignation and hostility that they have resort to every manner of subterfuge and evasion. They meet together to discuss plans for opposition and defense, form clubs for mutual support, and drink more now from very defiance than they ever did from inclination. And the liquor sellers struggle desperately to carry on the traffic in spite of the law. A business which has a profit of eight cents on every ten-cent drink is too good a one to give up without a strenuous effort.

Thousands of intelligent people, temperate and even total abstainers, do not uphold prohibition on principle; not because they are opposed to the cause of temperance, but they say that it is an infringement of individual liberty, both unjust and unconstitutional; that it has a tendency, also, to create law breakers, and to cultivate a general disrespect for all laws when they conflict with personal interests. Such conditions engender a hostile agitation and a spirit of unrest in the minds of the people.

There is probably no class of citizens who oppose prohibition more zealously than our foreign-born population, particularly the German portion. We have stated before the reasons for this, which ought to command the consideration of every unprejudiced advocate of temperance. Nor does all the injury of this coercive system fall alone on the parties whose liberties are abridged. There is a reactive effect, in nowise beneficial, felt by the prohibitionists themselves. They evince a violence of opposition that has often more of combativeness than of principle. In a late election in California so aggressive was this feeling that on several occasions it almost led to the commission of crime.

In summing up the foregoing facts on this subject, we arrive at the following conclusion: That prohibitory laws have not been a success in redeeming the drunkard, but they have branded him as a criminal. The calling of the seller of intoxicants has been rendered infamous, and both he and the consumer are classed in the same category with thieves and other disturbers of the peace. And of what crime are they guilty, since neither the selling or drinking of liquors is prohibited by the laws of the United States?

There is a movement now on foot in Maine to overthrow the prohibitory policy. It has its origin in Waldo County, and undoubtedly means the formation of a license law party. Those interested declare the present prohibitory law is subversive of the personal liberty of the citizen, is thoroughly impracticable in its principles, and is a violation of the most important provisions of the Constitution. There is every indication that this opinion but voices the sentiments of a large number of both Republican and

Democratic voters. The great preacher, Henry Ward Beecher, says:—

"Prohibitory laws are right in principle, but as they cannot be enforced it is useless to enact them. You may make regulations, but total prevention you can never have. Arguments used by temperance men are often absurd. They say that stimulants of every kind are bad, and that all kinds of alcoholic drinks are inevitable poisons. In trying to combat intemperance, physiology is a good weapon, good cooking is another, rational amusements another. If a man thinks it right to drink, he ought not to be denounced by those who do not. Calvin said to his students, 'Observe the Sabbath; but if any man says to you, you must keep it, then break it as a token of your Christian liberty.'

"The story that was gotten up, and is still in circulation, that the wine which our Saviour made at the marriage at Canaan was not fermented liquor, but fresh grape juice, is an example of the sacrifice of personal integrity to the interests of the church.

"There is reason to fear that the final result of the attempt to suppress the use of liquors by prohibition may be a relapse into a worse condition of things than prevailed before the temperance reform began."

CHAPTER XVI.

CAUSES OF INTEMPERANCE.

In discussing this branch of our subject we shall find it necessary to repeat the substance of former statements in order to impress certain things upon the mind of the reader.

The causes of intemperance may be treated under two heads, the esoteric and the exoteric. In considering the first we are bound to emphasize the vast importance of hereditary influences as being fruitful sources of a craving for intoxicants. Few parents realize that they transmit tastes and habits to their offspring along with a physical resemblance. In fact, these are often more marked than any facial likeness. Especially is this true of a love of stimulating liquors. The confirmed habit of the father or mother is, alas! too often a direct heritage to the child.

The desire for intoxicating drinks, thus transmitted, is often so powerful as to make the fight with it of life-long duration. A physician, eminent in the profession, once told me that so great was this inborn craving in him that as far back as he could remember the very odor of whisky would cause the saliva to stream from his mouth. Let it be said to the credit of this brave man that before he had reached maturity he made a solemn vow never to taste a drop of liquor, and kept it up to a hale and hearty old age.

Many physicians, honest in their belief, are frequently responsible for the cultivation of intemperate habits, by their practice of prescribing spirituous liquors for trivial complaints. Ninety-nine times out of a hundred, however, the patient would have fared better without it, and would also have been spared the curse of having acquired a craving for intoxicants that often results in his ruin.

Grief, despondency, loss of fortune or friend, nopeless love, unhappy marital relations, stimulating foods and condiments, excessive use of animal food, pastry, strong tea and coffee, particularly in persons of sedentary habits, all have a tendency to depress vitality and create a desire for alcoholic stimulants; any dejection of spirits, either from physical or mental causes, that induces a hopeless, pessimistic view of life, is apt to be followed by an intense longing for something that will give temporary relief. A man thus afflicted, naturally resorts to whisky, or some other alcoholic liquor, to drown his sensations, and enable him to forget himself for the time being. Derangement of the liver is often responsible for a large surplus of trouble in this world. A healthy stomach does not crave stimulants. A man with a good digestion is naturally cheerful. The state of the mind is an almost infallible guide as to the condition of the digestive organs. Our insane asylums are peopled by victims of dyspepsia, and thousands of unfortunates commit suicide every year from the same cause.

The exoteric causes of intemperance are better known to the majority of people, and are those combatted by advocates of total abstinence. Of these various causes, social customs are probably the most prolific source of immoderate drinking. Most men regard the common practice of treating to drinks a necessity to the proper greeting of a friend or acquaintance. The contiguity of the ubiquitous saloon furnishes the opportunity. This custom seems to be peculiar to Ireland and our country. In Germany a man pays for what he drinks, which is as it should be. A high-spirited man should esteem it an impertinence for another to propose to pay for his liquor. To entertain a friend in one's own house and to volunteer to pay for his entertainment in a saloon are very different things. The customs of society are tyrannical, and too often follow us through life, to our own detriment.

The love of conviviality so deeply implanted in most of us, is another great incentive to drinking habits. In the present condition of society it is an almost universal belief that one cannot show good-fellowship to one's friends without the offering of spirituous liquors. A man who is secretly opposed to this practice will often follow it rather than to subject himself to the suspicion of being niggardly or inhospitable.

It is frequently urged as a plea in favor of the use of alcohol by our public speakers, that their brilliancy and eloquence are enhanced by, and largely dependent upon, the glass of spirits taken before ascending the rostrum. This habit of Daniel Webster is a common illustration of the theory.

There is no doubt that so powerful a stimulant does away for the time being with all nervousness and trepidation, substituting a feeling of self-satisfaction and confidence. It is done, however, at the ultimate sacrifice of the integrity of the nervous system, and when the habit is confirmed, a man is pitiably dependent on it. How much better and braver it would be to live down the first natural timidity by the aid of the higher stimulant of a determined will to "speak right on" that which we know will be of benefit to our hearers. A man who is "drunk with conviction," as Emerson says, will not fail to be more eloquent in his earnestness than he who is drunk on whisky. Better to follow such examples as Henry Grattan, the illustrious Irish barrister and statesman, and the renowned Disraeli, both of whom made failures of their maiden speeches, than voluntarily to be placed under the dominion of that insatiable despot, Alcohol.

The principal incentive to drunkenness is the saloons, and in their suppression we are heart and soul with the prohibitionists. They are a crying evil in the land, and harm both those who keep them and the luckless beings who enter their accursed doors. They are dens of infamy, hot-beds of cruelty, prostitution and every order of crime known to unhappy humanity.

It is well known that saloons are often the rendezvous of the worst characters, who meet to devise plans to prey on the community; that a majority of the homicides and assaults are committed in these places; that they are schools of depravity and nurseries of licentiousness, where, under the influence of spirituous liquors, all the baser passions are excited. They are the natural home of the striker, and the repeater at elections, and frauds against the sanctity of the ballot are too often concocted within their doors.

The granting of licenses to these way-stations on the road to poverty and a drunkard's grave, is a wrong against every man, woman and child in the community. It is an act not guided by wisdom or a proper regard for the morals and well-being of the people. A Government should do all in its power to promote morality and further that which is of vital import to the nation; and in this licensing of saloons our laws have but opened the way to every kind of immorality and crime.

It is also the duty of a Government to protect the weak and remove as far as possible all temptations from the people which could encourage intemperance or any other injurious custom. For this reason, if for no other, it is wrong to grant licenses to persons whose pecuniary interest is to pander to habits which lead to drunkenness. And to legislate the wretched victim of such a system into jails along with criminals and law-breakers for what the Supreme Court of the State of New York has decided is not a crime, is the very crown of this wrong to humanity.

The present system of granting licenses is also an evidence of legalized inconsistency. It cannot reform the drunkard. It makes the selling of liquor lawful, while rendering both the tempter and the tempted culprits in the eyes of the law. Looking at the question even from a business standpoint we fail to see wherein saloons are of practical benefit to the people. The amount of money paid into the treasury for their licenses cannot compensate them for the immense sums spent in the prosecution of crimes that had their origin in these places. Therefore on no ground whatsoever are local authorities justified in granting saloon licenses for the sale of spirituous liquors.

In advocating the suppression of saloons we wish it distinctly understood that this does not include the prohibition of the manufacture and sale of spirituous beverages of any kind. These industries should be free under proper governmental regulations. Our object is to prevent the sale of spirituous liquors and fortified wines to be drunk on the premises where they are sold.

CHAPTER XVII.

REMEDIES SUGGESTED FOR INTEMPERANCE.

In proposing remedies for the esoteric causes of intemperance we direct special attention to the fact that breeders of horses and other animals take an infinite amount of pains to observe and carry out the law of heredity. It is lamentable that equal judgment and foresight are not used in propagating the human species, which is certainly a matter of far graver consequence to mankind. A man may be excused for being indifferent to the quality of colts and lambs that he raises, but it is not so easy to overlook a thoughtlessness as to the kind of children he brings into the world.

A practical application of this law on behalf of human beings would be an immense factor in the ultimate progress of the race. Its effect would be evident in a single generation, and its persistence through succeeding ones would be productive of incalculable improvement to man. His instincts would become simpler and purer, and his appetites be subordinate to his spiritual perception. So many excellent works are devoted to the elucidation of this subject that it is not necessary to do more in these pages than to impress upon the reader the importance of making a thorough research into hereditary influences.

> "The man is ignorant of law who gives
> Being to offspring, cursed, before their birth,
> With passions that destroy their future peace,
> And make the stately fabric of the soul
> A dungeon of impure depravities."

A man or woman who is addicted to habits of inebriety is unfitted to become a parent, and if offspring be born of such they are almost inevitably afflicted with an insatiate longing for some kind of stimulant. Sad indeed is the case where a father or mother is responsible for a life-long misery to a child! It is not in human nature for the latter to regard with perfect filial love and respect the author of a hereditary vice in himself, and his seeming ingratitude is based on a just appreciation of what he realizes has been defrauded him by birth.

There is probably no more effective cure for intemperance than the adoption of a strictly vegetarian diet. It is a natural law that the human system craves most that which it feeds upon. The man who lives principally on animal flesh is not equally satisfied with other kinds of food, because the tissues of his body are composed of that material; while to the vegetarian such a diet would be distasteful or positively obnoxious.

Animal foods, particularly those which are called red meats, such as beef, mutton and pork, are very stimulating, whereas cereals, fruits and vegetables are not at all so. There is an intimate relationship between both solid and fluid stimulants. Persons addicted to the use of ardent spirits are almost invariably lovers of rich foods, and the ranks of the inebriate are generally supplied from high livers. A vegetarian is seldom, *if ever,* given to intoxicants.

If a vegetable diet be adopted for a sufficient length of time, the old tissue of the body will be eliminated, and new tissue will be evolved from the non-stimulating foods to take its place; the desire for liquor will gradually decrease with this change of tissue.

Physicians should teach people that the effect of a stimulant is always evanescent and usually leaves an increased longing for its repetition; that the continuance of such use *must* terminate in a lessening of vital power, in a deadening of the finer attributes of our nature, and a general tendency to grossness, with a slow but positive overthrow of spiritual insight and power.

A man is always cleaner, purer, manlier and more self-possessed when absolutely uninfluenced by spirituous beverages. They unfit him for the society of ladies, and are a common bar to domestic felicity, for, as a rule, women prefer the caresses of a man whose breath is untainted by liquor.

The various discussions on temperance in communities have had the excellent result of putting drinking habits in disfavor among the educated classes. It is no longer a joking matter to see a man under the influence of liquor, for people have grown to regard such a sight as most unpleasant and pitiable. No one now need fear being thought singular or unsocial if he refuses to drink with a friend, and a man is universally held in respect who has the manhood to declare his principles and live up to them.

We now come to the consideration of a remedy for the most formidable of all the sources of intemperance—the saloons. With regard to the power of States to prevent by legal enactments the establishing and keeping of such places of resort, we submit the following decisions of the Supreme Court of the United States.

Justice Taney says: "If any State deems the retail and internal traffic in ardent spirits injurious to its citizens, and calculated to produce idleness, vice or debauchery, I see nothing in the Constitution of the United States to prevent it from regulating, restraining, or prohibiting altogether, if it thinks proper."

Justice Catron further asserts: "If the State has the power of restraint by license to any extent, she has the discriminating power to judge of its limits, and may go the length of prohibiting altogether." And other justices concur in the opinion of Justice Grier, when he positively declares: "It is not necessary to array the appalling statistics of misery, pauperism and crime which have their origin in the abuse of ardent spirits; and to correct these great evils, all measures of restraint or prohibition necessary to effect that purpose are legitimately within the power of the State Government."

The question now arises, Would it be a wise procedure to suddenly close these establishments? It is true that a majority of them are disreputable, but there are some that are frequented by a thoroughly respectable class of citizens who meet there for friendly association, and a peremptory shutting off of this privilege would evoke loud complaints on their part. The customs of a people cannot be abruptly changed. Time, growth and education are important factors in a permanent reformation.

At the same time it would be the height of folly to expect men to improve in their drinking habits while saloons are licensed to sell that which produces drunkenness. A great step in the right direction would be to alter the character of these saloon licenses, so that they prohibit the sale of *spirituous* liquors and *fortified wines*, and allowing only *pure wines, beer and cider* to be sold by them. Although preferring the total prohibition of saloons if it could be effected without such positive objections on the part of the masses, we think the next best thing would be this change in the general system of liquor licenses. Massachusetts has five distinct classes; the second, fourth and fifth read as follows:—

"To grant licenses to sell malt liquors, cider and light wines to be drunk *on* the premises.

"To grant licenses for the sale of alcoholic liquors of all kinds *not* to be drunk on the premises.

"To grant licenses to sell malt liquors, cider and light wines *not* to be drunk on the premises."

These licenses, if honestly enforced, would result in a diminution of drunkenness in a very short space of time. This course could not elicit serious opposition from either the advocates of total abstinence, or of those who practice moderate indulgence. The latter, by not being compelled to forego his glass, would lend a more willing adherence to the support of any law that would mitigate the curse of intemperance, the evil effects of which both admit.

The adoption of such a system of licensing would go far to disarm the antagonism of the saloon-keepers and their supporters, and would aid in undermining the powerful organizations of the liquor dealers. The strength of the latter is developed in proportion to the opposition they receive. The people generally would not be aroused to violent resistance because they would be permitted to procure liquor when they wished it, just so they drank it off the premises where they are sold.

The past thirty years' experience with our present licensing system, proves its inefficiency to render much assistance to the cause of temperance. It would hardly seem wise, therefore, to persist in a course so unproductive of permanent benefit. The universality of alcoholic drinking among all peoples makes any sudden change by repressive laws, an impossibility. We must depend upon the slower but surer processes of wise legislation that will restrict and control, rather than coerce.

A man can only attain his highest development by leaving his actions perfectly untrammeled. Liberty of choice should always be open to him. He cannot progress under duress. This is in harmony with the divine plan. His wrong-doing is an experience by which he learns wisdom; the events of another's life can never be his guide to knowledge. Therefore, great as is the evil of excessive indulgence in alcoholic liquors, they must not be arbitrarily withheld from him.

The eliminating of whisky and other spirituous mixtures from the saloon-keeper's list of supplies, would be like extracting the poisonous fangs from the adder.

Various regulations could be adopted that would assist in educating the people to pay less attention to the mere act of drinking, and more to the opportunity for social converse. The ordinary American method of taking a drink *standing* before the bar of a saloon has not the redeeming social features of the German "Bier Garten" or French "Café." In these attractive places you invite your friend to a table where lunch, or tobacco with pipes, is the customary concomitant of the liquor served, and all are but recognized additions to the pleasure of mutual companionship. It is certainly a far less objectionable and more dignified manner of drinking than what we daily witness in this country.

The keepers of saloons must be deterred from underhand practices to defraud the law, by the strict enforcement of exemplary penalties for its violation.

The strongest opposition to any change in the licensing system would come from large cities and towns; but the population throughout the country and villages would outvote the cities.

The subject of local option which we have previously considered under the operation of coercive laws, would now be just and equitable under the principle of regulation. Communities have the right to protect the morals of the people, and are justified in prohibiting any business which they believe encourages dissolute habits, just as they would abate a public nuisance. No one's personal liberty is abridged thereby, for a man is not debarred from purchasing whatsoever liquor he wishes, as he would be under total prohibition.

In the new *regime* special regulations could be made for hotels, restaurants, theaters and other places of amusement and recreation. The first two should not be deprived of the privilege of supplying their guests with liquors, to be sold in bottles and sent to their own rooms, but bars should be prohibited. What constitutes a hotel or a restaurant should be clearly defined, so as not to include lodging-houses in rights that would constantly lead to violation.

Theaters and other places of a similar character where it is customary to furnish members of the audience with liquor during the performance on the stage should not be prohibited from continuing the custom, only confining the drinks to light wines, beer, etc.

Suburban parks, and other places of public resort, where rifle-shooting and various amusements are enjoyed, should have like regulations.

Club-houses ought to be regarded as having equal rights with a private residence and so be exempt from any interference with their rules. Public dinners and social entertainments should not be debarred from any privilege enjoyed by the individual.

Other exceptions to the general observance of liquor regulations may arise, which will require special ordinances as time develops them. Temperance coffee-houses and places of amusement would be a great assistance to the eradication of drinking habits. It is impossible to specify the minutiæ concerned in the practical application of this proposed revision of the license law. Our position here must be suggestive rather than assertive. We would, however, emphasize the necessity of utterly excluding the element of coercion from this or any other reformation.

We leave to wiser heads than ours the formulating of suitable plans under the new dispensation for the gradual changing of intemperate customs and habits among the people, only stipulating that no member of the commonwealth be deprived of a single personal right or privilege.

In conclusion, we urge the importance of cultivating all the amenities of life which will directly or indirectly encourage an abhorrence of intoxicants. No opportunity should be lost of impressing upon the tender minds of the young the utter beastliness of drunkenness. A child should be taught to regard with horror anything that could even for a moment rob him of his self-control.

CHAPTER XVIII.

THE ADVANTAGES OF AN INCREASED PRODUCTION OF WINE AND BEER.

In previous chapters in this work we have shown that in all European countries where wine is the common drink of the masses, intoxication was of infrequent occurrence until the wine crop fell short and adulterations were resorted to by the manufacturers. These spurious compounds were principally made from corn and potato spirits, which, from their poisonous properties, created an unnatural craving for stimulants in those persons who drank them. Drunkenness now became common, and from these facts we must reason that if pure wines were again placed on the market, and adulteration were made a crime punishable by law in every country, the people would be led to use more wine, which means less whisky and brandy, and consequently less intoxication.

No valid objection can be raised against the moderate drinking of pure wine any more than the eating of stimulating foods, like roast beef, eggs, etc. It is the excess of such use that should be avoided as being both gluttonous and harmful.

The enormous production of wine in European countries demonstrates its extensive use among the nations of the earth, and its vast importance as an industry. The vineyards in some districts extend over immense areas of land, giving employment to thousands of men, women, and children. Millions of capital are invested in the wine manufacture, thus furnishing work for thousands more. In comprehending the extent of the almost limitless interests at stake in the carrying on of the various branches of labor connected with grape culture, wine-making, and wine traffic in general, we can see how useless would be the attempt to exterminate it. Coercive laws could not crush these interests nor do much to change the habits of the millions of people who drink wine. The wisest course would be to give them pure wine instead of the poisonous adulterations now sold for such.

The climate of California is peculiarly adapted to the cultivation of the grape. In 1862 there was considerable excitement about the vineyard possibilities of this State, and many varieties of grapes were planted, but were uprooted some ten years later and fruit trees substituted. Seven years ago there was a revival of grape culture in California, which was carefully fostered by the new State Board of Viticulture. At that time there were only thirty-five thousand acres of vines in the entire State, eighty per cent of which were of poor quality. To-day there are one hundred and fifty thousand acres, ninety per cent of which are foreign varieties of wine, table and raisin grapes, making an investment of over $65,000,000.

It is not an exaggeration, therefore, to assert that

not many years will elapse before California's vine interests will outrank those of any other country on the globe, and her people will be given a permanent and remunerative source of employment. The earlier ripening of the grape on this coast opens an almost unlimited market for this fruit in the Eastern States. The remaining quantities not used by home consumption, or the making of raisins, will be turned into our wine presses, thus furnishing vast revenues to our people.

In the cultivation of the vines and the gathering of the grapes, men, women and children would be given light and healthful employment. Machinists, coopers, bottle-makers, in fact all the employes in branches of labor connected with this industry, would receive an impetus that would give new life to trade, commerce and civilization.

Instead of thousands of acres being devoted to vineyards, hundreds of thousands will be thus utilized in the near future, bringing comparative wealth to numberless homes throughout our hills and valleys. This ease from delving toil will be followed by an inevitable increase of wealth, intellectual culture, refinement of tastes and manners, more elegant private structures, art galleries, museums, churches, theaters, baths, etc., that are the natural outcome of an æsthetic and prosperous people. Schiller believed that man would be regenerated through the influence of the beautiful.

Under the principles of this great republic the masses will rise with this wave of fortune, and California will enjoy an era far more brilliant and substantial than the famous golden one of forty-nine.

To effect such grand results the most stringent laws should be enforced to prevent the decoction of poisonous liquors to be sold as wine. Then whisky will no longer be the national drink. Its slaves will cease to exist, for this now mighty monarch will be forever dethroned by the joyous god of pure wine. All internal revenue tax should be removed from the latter and every facility given for its cheap manufacture and sale.

In a letter from the Mayor of Jérez de la Frontera, the capital of the sherry district, to the American Consul at Cadiz, the following pertinent statement is made:—

"The condition of the wine market is deplorable. Purchases of real sherry are now very seldom made. The conditions of the industry have wholly changed, and the vineyards which represent so much capital, have now little value. More wine is exported as sherry than the whole district produces, while the legitimate product has no sale. The importation of German alcohol into Cadiz for the production of this spurious sherry is increasing steadily. Distilled chiefly from the beet and potato, it is inferior to Spanish alcohol, and has driven the latter and all other alcohols out of the Spanish market."

It is known that similar adulterations to those in Spain are carried on in all other wine countries in Europe, and it is not to be wondered at that intemperance is more prevalent among these people than formerly. No action would be more effective in destroying this culpable business than the production of pure wines brought within the means of the masses by the removal of all burdens of taxation from its manufacture. A healthful article could be made here and sold at lower rates than it would be possible to procure adulterated compounds from Europe with the cost of transportation added.

Arpad Haraszthy, President of the State Board of Viticultural Commissioners, read a paper entitled, "How to Drink Wine." "Wine," he said, "should never be drunk except at table, and then only in moderate quantities. The character of the food should also harmonize with the wine used. Then, again, personal disposition should be studied in the matter. A person of a phlegmatic disposition should drink white wines, which promote both physical and mental activity. People of nervous and excitable temperaments should confine themselves to clarets and red wines, which are slow to affect the nervous system, and tend to soothe both body and mind. People with a superabundance of blood should carefully avoid red and fortified wines."

The San Francisco *Chronicle* of April 18, 1887, says: "Charles Kohler, the pioneer of viticulture in California, who died suddenly of apoplexy yesterday, was a strong advocate of temperance. He pointed with pride to the fact that drunkenness is a crime almost unknown in wine-growing countries, and he looked forward with confidence to the moral and social advantages which would follow when California's pure wines shall have performed their mission of crowding out strong, spirituous liquors in general."

Although it is commonly admitted that the drinking of beer, porter, etc., has not the same refining influence as is accredited to wine, yet they are far less injurious than spirituous mixtures. Pure malt liquors, from the small amount of alcohol they contain, can hardly be esteemed inimical to sobriety. If unadulterated, they should be placed in the same category as pure wines, and be subject to like regulations. An English journal says: "Were the brewing trade completely free, that is, every vestige of the licensing system abolished, there would be the same keen competition in this business that there is in other departments of industry; and it would be quite as impossible for the brewers to maintain their prices at a forced elevation as it is for the bakers and butchers to artificially enhance the price of bread and beef." And Mr. Cobden, the promoter of the abolition of the corn laws in England in 1864, declares that the case of the British agriculturalist, who, "after raising a bushel of barley, is compelled to pay a tax of sixty per cent before he is permitted to convert it into a beverage for his own consumption, is an injustice that would never be tolerated by cultivators of olives and grapes in France and Italy."

The price of beer is thus greatly increased, not only by the duties, but also by the vexatious and endless restrictions laid on its preparation and sale. This enhanced price leads to the consumption of gin and other spirituous liquors, that are much worse in their consequences."

The German Government, knowing that malt liquors were the habitual beverage used by the people, nurtured the growth and the manufacture of beer. The result is, that the Germans as a nation are temperate, industrious and contented, and in no other country is drunkenness less prevalent. Public sentiment there is intolerant of this vice.

The brewing interests in America have attained a magnitude and power equally dangerous with those of distilled liquors. Take away the internal revenue tax on both, and you virtually annihilate the liquor rings. There could not possibly be trusts or monopolies under free brewing and distilling.

Governments cannot more effectually discharge their duties than by a careful investigation of this subject, for on the proper regulation of liquor laws the success of the cause of temperance largely depends.

CHAPTER XIX.

ALCOHOL AS A FACTOR IN HUMAN PROGRESS.

WHEN we consider the vast number of substances disseminated throughout every clime from which alcohol can be subtracted, the conclusion is inevitable that the Creator intended it for wise and useful purposes in the progress and elevation of man. Everything in nature is adapted to his use, whether in its natural state or in the various commodities manufactured under his intelligent supervision. All the laws of the universe, when properly understood, are seen to be beneficently ministering to the physical, intellectual and spiritual growth of God's chief handiwork, man. Alcohol cannot be an exception, for it is of immense advantage to the human race, though esteemed a curse by many who have not a proper conception of its utility.

It is a matter of interest and profit to study the multitudinous uses to which this spirit is applied, and learn its absolute necessity in the material advancement of the arts, sciences and industries of a civilized people. In the laboratory of the chemist, alcohol is one of the most essential articles. As a heat-producer, a re-agent and a solvent of numerous substances, it is indispensable in his experiments.

With the pharmaceutist it is a necessary and expensive ingredient in his preparations of medicinal tinctures and compounds; and the physician finds it impossible without alcohol to preserve morbid specimens taken from the living or the deceased body. In the manufacture of a majority of patent medicines it is the most costly material employed, some establishments demanding as high as 50,000 gallons of alcohol yearly in making a single article.

Painters use thousands of gallons annually in their work, especially in the production of varnish, as it is a ready solvent of the resinous substances of which this finish is composed. Alcohol is a necessity in preparing certain favorite dyes, and hat manufacturers require large quantities for the dissolving of the gums by which the bodies of silk hats are stiffened for the outside covering. It is in great demand in the manufacture of perfumeries, and in the preparation of anæsthetics such as chloroform and various ethers, in which it is the principal ingredient. For domestic purposes it has been found a convenient generator of heat. In fact, so general is the utility of this spirit that its use can hardly be overestimated.

In the distillation of alcohol what is called proof spirit is a mixture of fifty per cent of alcohol with an equal proportion of water by weight. This is the spirit from which whisky is manufactured, and on which a tax of ninety cents a gallon is paid. The cost to the manufacturer is about twenty cents a gallon and the tax added brings it up to $1.10. It takes nearly two gallons of proof spirit to make one of commercial alcohol, which contains nearly ninety per cent of alcohol and ten per cent of water, and therefore has a tax nearly double that put upon proof spirit. This would bring the cost of alcohol to the distiller to about $2.20 a gallon, whereas the price less the tax would actually be about forty cents.

The income derived by the United States Government from this tax of ninety cents a gallon averages annually about $60,000,000. It is estimated that only about half of this proof spirit is made into whisky, the other half being converted into commercial alcohol, which is consumed in the arts, sciences and various industries above stated. Thus $30,000,000 is paid to the Government every year by the people for the privilege of drinking whisky, and $30,000,000 additional tax is paid by them in articles they purchase, which require alcohol in their composition or manufacture.

It must be that this matter has never been properly presented to the people; that they do not comprehend its direct import, or such a monstrous injustice could not have existed so long.

During the war, and for some years afterwards, it is easy to understand that there was a necessity for such taxation, but at the present time, with an overflowing treasury, steps should be taken for its immediate removal. It is a very suggestive fact that distillers do not desire the removal of this tax; they well know that it would destroy the monopoly which they now have in the liquor traffic. Thus it is that every man, woman and child in the United States is taxed —for what? Mainly to increase the cost of liquors, in the vain hope of preventing a few miserable drunkards from overindulgence. Is such an impost just to the people, or is it statesmanlike in our lawgivers to continue it on our statute books?

It is a recognized law of trade that the cheapening of an article increases its sale. Generally speaking this is true, and it is a common argument that the abolition of the tax would reduce the price of liquor to the extent of encouraging drunkenness. Whisky, however, seems to be an exception to this law, for the reason that inordinate desire on the part of the individual forces him to obtain it, no matter what it costs. As an elucidation of this fact we quote from an article published some months ago in the San Francisco *Chronicle*, which had the following excerpt from a report made to Congress about the year 1869, by the well-known statistician, David A. Wells, on the propriety of reducing the tax on distilled spirits:—

"Everyone knows that the appetite for alcoholic drinks is not restrained by the question of their cost, and that consequently cheap whisky would be no more hostile to prohibition than dear whisky; whereas expensive alcohol must necessarily restrict in a great degree those products of which it is an essential element. We are a great deal more apt to economize in our necessities than in our luxuries; it is human nature to do without the things we need in order that we may have the things we want. For this reason, prohibition cuts no figure in this sort of discussion."

In the same article we find the following relevant opinion of Charles Heber Clark:—

"Total extinction of the whisky tax," he argues, "would not reduce the price of whisky at retail and would not make one more drunkard. Doubling the whisky tax would not increase the retail price and would not keep a single tippler sober. The English Government taxes liquors so heavily that it depends upon them for one-fourth of its entire revenue, and it is admitted by intelligent observers that there is more drunkenness in England than in any other civilized country on the globe. The whisky distillers of this country, who surely have no motive for desiring decreased consumption, are unanimous in opposition to the removal of the tax. The tax upon distilled spirits is not a special tax upon whisky-drinkers and saloon-keepers; but it is a direct tax upon the entire population of the country, drunk or sober. The fact is kept in the background that alcohol made from distilled spirits is an essential and important branch of American industry.

"The people pay this tax when they buy the products of a number of industries. They pay it when they use perfumery, when they take chloroform, and when they consume drugs. The suffering poor man pays it when he goes to the apothecary to cure himself of the cold caught by his exclusion from the privilege of enfolding himself in a British blanket. He pays it when he puts bay-rum on his hair, when he buys cologne for his wife's handkerchief, and when he lays in paregoric for his baby. It covers his head when he puts on an American hat. He sits on it when he drops into an American varnished chair. The tax is on honest and decent industry, and that is a good reason why it should be taken off. The attempt to use the sentiment for temperance in an effort to help the distillers to have the tax retained is an affront to public intelligence."

The cost of commercial alcohol to the consumer at the present time is about $2.50 a gallon; subtract the tax, and it could be sold at from sixty to seventy-five cents a gallon. Now, supposing this tax removed, what would be the result? It would have the general effect of cheapening every article whose production depends upon this spirit. To the professor of chemistry this reduction would be a great boon, enabling him to experiment more freely in the interest of science than he could possibly do with alcohol at its present figure. It would be a considerable aid also to the poor student in his efforts to master this wonderful science, and the benefit that would accrue to the pharmaceutist in his preparations of tinctures, etc., and doctor's prescriptions, can hardly be appreciated.

The abolition of this tax would reduce the cost of patent medicines to a minimum; and when we consider the enormous consumption of these compounds in America alone, we can form some conception of the immense saving this cheapening would be to the people. Then, again, such a step would be a direct incentive to the universal progress of the arts, so lessening the price of their products as to place them within easy reach of many more purchasers. Painters are large consumers of alcohol, and in the manufacture of varnish alone, the saving in the cost of this article would enable them to work profitably at greatly reduced rates, thus insuring an increased patronage.

The employment of anæsthetics in which alcohol is the principal ingredient, has become so extensive that a reduction of their price would be a saving to both physician and patient.

In the making of perfumery, especially cologne, the cheapening of alcohol will put these delightful compounds in the possession of a much larger proportion of our population than can possibly afford them at their present cost. Their extensive use would be no insignificant factor in the cultivation of more esthetic tastes and habits.

Lessening the price of an article not only increases its consumption, but as a consequence its manufacture must also be stimulated; thus thousands of working men and women would be given employment and thereby insured the comforts of life.

The extra amount of money put in circulation by this activity in certain industries would greatly encourage both local and general trade. Not only this, but indirectly all business interests would feel the impetus, for trades of every kind are so cemented that each is affected more or less by activity or depression in any prominent one.

Then again the increased production of alcohol to meet the demand would necessitate more grain for its manufacture, which would be a direct advantage to the farmer. As a consequence it would bring into cultivation thousands of acres of land that are now unvexed by the plow, with a probable enhancement of the price of grain; thus, in divers ways, augmenting the prosperity of the people, and surrounding them with all the corollaries that wealth can supply.

In addition to the reasons before stated for abolishing the revenue tax such a step would do away with illicit distillation and thus eliminate from the community a large number of law-breakers that are a constant annoyance to the people surrounding the stills. It would also undermine whisky rings, as before said, which are an unmitigated disgrace to the country.

CHAPTER XX.

TO PROHIBITIONISTS.

The liquor problem and the temperance question have engaged the attention of statesmen for centuries past, but more especially have they been agitated in the last fifty years. Every plan of specific licensing and prohibition that human intellect could formulate, has been successively tried to regulate the traffic and stem the torrent of intemperance. The failure of each in turn proves some inherent defect to exist in these various methods. A law based on justice and equity is far more apt to meet the approval of the people than one which wholly or partially ignores these principles; and that the present licensing system and prohibitory laws are not founded on justice and equity, we trust we have made plain in preceding chapters.

To establish a right conception of our subject, and to remove erroneous impressions, we have devoted a portion of this work to the history of fermented and spirituous liquors, their physiological, therapeutic and toxicological action on the human system, their use and abuse, the many purposes for which alcohol is a necessity, the universality of alcoholic beverages, and the fact that intemperance in all nations is coeval with their manufacture.

It is a matter of importance that should be noted by prohibitionists that intemperance has become a national curse in great Britain and America, where the most strenuous efforts have been made to prevent it, whereas in European countries there are no license or prohibitory laws; and yet there is comparatively little drunkenness among the people.

Repressive laws have now been in operation in this country for over thirty years, without appreciably abating the great evil. In summing up their practical results we find that they have aroused the bitterest antagonism among individuals and parties, been the direct cause of innumerable evasions and deceptions, created law-breakers, and generally educated the masses in habits of thought inimical to the constituted authorities. No law which creates such disturbance in the mental atmosphere of a people, can be productive of good.

Advocates of prohibition not only attempt to suppress intemperance by coercive laws, but also to compel temperate drinkers to become total abstainers by prohibiting the manufacture and sale of all liquors. This general inclusion is unavoidable because the law can make no individual distinction, but its effect is unfortunately adverse to the intention of its founders.

The man who occasionally takes a glass of liquor is forced into a position of antagonism to the believer in total abstinence, whereas they are in reality friends, and would work in harmony were it not for the coercive measures above stated. It is not wise to alienate one's friends in any of the relations of life. A combination of the forces of these two opposers of drunkenness, would result in a rapid advance of temperance habits among the people. In removing the cause of their difference, you at once command the support of the majority of voters in every State in the Union, for most of these men are addicted to the use of liquor of some kind.

To the reconciliation of these two great enemies of intemperance, every philanthropic mind should direct its keenest energies.

Is it not time, therefore, that some other plan be adopted which will better harmonize with the love of justice and freedom, deep-rooted in the hearts of a civilized nation? A bad law makes rebellious citizens. No law at all is better than one which interferes with the sacredness of personal liberty by compelling a man not to do what cannot be regarded as a wrong in itself. Such legislation must always fall short of its object.

The prohibition party is acknowledged to be a disintegrating element in our politics of to-day, and in the coming campaign much that is relative to this question depends on the course taken by them. In no small degree they hold the balance of power between the two great political parties that rule the destinies of the country. Their responsibility at this immediate time, is the gravest and most potential.

To stop the drinking habits of people is not the only question which should engage their attention, to the exclusion of every other. It is not a matter of more importance in a community to legislate for the drunkard than for the sober man. In our zeal to reform the drunkard, we must not lose sight of the legitimate interests of the temperate man. The business success of the latter often requires large quantities of alcohol, and any increase in its price is of vital moment to him. The products of his manufactory supply a definite want in the community, or they would not meet so ready a sale. The revenue necessary for the support of the Government should be collected from those things which are articles of luxury, as much as possible avoiding the taxation of essential products. Where an article is used in both capacities its general character must be determined before deciding whether it should be taxed or not. As, for instance, the use of opium as a luxury far outbalances its employment medicinally, and consequently its taxation is in accordance with its principal demand.

Distilled spirits, in the state in which it leaves the still, cannot possibly be esteemed an article of luxury. No one ever drinks pure alcohol, and yet before it can undergo the various processes essential to make it into whisky it is taxed ninety cents on a gallon. Prohibitionists are too apt to assume that the greatest use to which alcohol is put, is that of a stealer of men's brains, whereas the truth of the matter is that not one-half of the spirits made are employed in beverages at all, the remainder being of necessity used in the arts, manufactures, etc. Some estimate may be had of the amount of this taxation from the fact that the chemist pays about $96 for a forty-six-gallon barrel of alcohol, which, without the tax, would cost him $20, or thereabouts.

The removal of this tax on distillations would lift

an enormous burden from many manufactures and cheapen the price to the consumer of numerous articles of utility, while it is safe to say that it would not decrease the retail price of liquor to any appreciable extent. Under our present system we are taxing the producer of articles of necessity for the benefit of the dispenser of an article of luxury. Our prohibition friends would do well to remember this and also the fact that a high revenue tax bears lightly on the saloon-keeper and heavily on the scientist and artisan, who must employ alcohol in their business.

Then again, if it were possible to close up all the distilleries in the United States, whisky would still be manufactured. Illicit distillation would be secretly carried on in the hills, mountains and obscure places all over the land, and no power of the Government could prevent it.

We have shown in a preceding chapter the importance of the wine industry, which is bound to become a source of incalculable wealth, notwithstanding all opposition. It is impossible to legislate new habits into the world. They are the outgrowth of successive generations, and will no doubt be inherited, in a measure, by our posterity for hundreds of years to come. That universal temperance will one day be achieved by our race, we have every reason to hope and expect. It must, however, be effected by slow processes. Man, like all other things in nature, must *grow* into perfection. No human law can immediately eradicate the desire for liquor in a confirmed whisky-tippler, for there is no regenerative power in the principle of force.

Intelligent beings must have the free exercise of their faculties and proclivities, even though their tendencies are not always for the right. Evil can only be cast out by an inborn desire for good. The province of a law is not to coerce a man, but to protect society from the wrong-doer.

While admitting the great good that temperance societies, especially the Women's Christian Temperance Union, have done, and are doing, for the young, we are sorry to say their combined efforts have not accomplished the reformation of the confirmed drunkard.

The enormous amount of money expended annually for liquor, and the untold misery resulting from habits of drunkenness, have been persistently explained to the people from both the pulpit and rostrum. Even the eloquent appeals of a Gough or Ingersoll have too often fallen upon barren soil and borne little fruit. Probably the English language does not contain a more graphic denunciation of the horrors of intemperance than is found in Mr. Ingersoll's address to a jury in a case where the question of alcohol was involved. We quote a portion of it here:—

"I do not believe that anybody can contemplate the subject without becoming prejudiced against the liquor crime. All we have to do is to think of the wrecks on either bank of the stream of death,—of the suicides, of the insanity, of the poverty, of the ignorance, of the destitution of the little children tugging at the faded and weary breasts of mothers, of weeping and despairing wives asking for bread, of the talented men of genius that it has wrecked, of those struggling with imaginary serpents, produced by this devilish thing; when you think of the jails, of the almshouses, of the asylums, of the prisons, of the scaffolds upon either bank, I do not wonder that every thoughtful man is prejudiced against this damned stuff that is called alcohol. Intemperance cuts down youth in its vigor, manhood in its strength, and age in its weakness. It breaks the father's heart, bereaves the doting mother, extinguishes natural affection, erases conjugal loves, blots out filial attachment, blights parental hope and brings down mourning age in sorrow to the grave. It produces weakness, not strength; sickness, not health; death, not life. It makes wives, widows; children, orphans; fathers, fiends; and all of them paupers and beggars. It feeds rheumatism, nurses gout, welcomes epidemics, invites cholera, imports pestilence and embraces consumption. It covers the land with idleness, misery and crime. It fills your jails, supplies your almshouses and demands your asylums. It engenders controversies, fosters quarrels and cherishes riots. It crowds your penitentiaries and furnishes victims for your scaffolds. It is the life-blood of the gambler, the element of the burglar, the prop of the highwayman and the support of the midnight incendiary. It countenances the liar, respects the thief, esteems the blasphemer and honors infamy. It defames benevolence, hates love, scorns virtue and slanders innocence. It incites the father to butcher his helpless offspring, helps the husband to massacre his wife, and the child to grind the parricidal ax.

"It burns up men, consumes women, detests life, curses God, and despises Heaven. It suborns witnesses, nurses perjury, defies the jury box and stains the judicial ermine. It degrades the citizen, debases the legislator, dishonors the statesman, and disarms the patriot. It brings shame, not honor; terror, not safety; despair, not hope; misery, not happiness; and with the malevolence of a fiend, it calmly surveys its frightful desolation, and, unsatisfied with its havoc, it poisons felicity, kills peace, ruins morals, blights confidence, slays reputation, and wipes out national honor; then curses the world and laughs at its ruin. It does all that and more—it murders the soul. It is the son of all villains, and the father of all crimes; the mother of abominations, the devil's best friend and God's worst enemy."

The second plank in the prohibition platform must meet the hearty approval of every advocate of temperance. We herewith insert it:—

"That the accursed liquor traffic is the gigantic 'crime of crimes' of our age, nation, state and country, desolating our homes, corrupting public morals, and sweeping millions of our race into the drunkard's grave and to the drunkard's doom, and should be forever banished from the land and from the world."

Such a consummation is most earnestly to be desired, but we have no faith in this being effected by the present platform of the prohibition party.

It is not sufficiently expansive for it ever to become a truly national party; as it now stands it can be, at best, but fractional and sporadic. Its influence can never sweep like a tidal wave over the public mind as did that of the Republican party in anti-slavery times. The secret of the latter's power was that its governing principle was the grand one of universal liberty. Such a battle-cry gathered conquering hosts around its standard. The shibboleth of the prohibitionist, on the contrary, embraces the opposite meaning—the infringement of individual rights and the subjugation of the whole people to his autocratic will.

It has been used as an argument by prohibitionists that as chattel slavery was uprooted by the sovereign power of the people, intemperance could be similarly destroyed. This does not follow, however. Slavery was upheld by an organized Government, and to effect its overthrow and establish human liberty, it was necessary to use force of arms. The position of the prohibitionist is not a parallel one; his object is the abridgment of personal rights and not the championship of individual liberty.

In view of what we have said in the preceding pages, and with the acknowledgment that all coercive laws for the prevention of drunkenness have been failures, it would seem the height of folly for prohibitionists to still continue in the same course. Their present system but intensifies one of the most important attributes in man's nature—the resistance to force, however applied.

We have advocated the closing of saloons; we still do so, but doubt its policy at the present time. This course may seem inconsistent with a desire to promote temperance; but, on the contrary, if the sale of *spirituous liquors* were prohibited in these places—which would be perfectly legitimate—it would be an immense step toward their total suppression. This system of regulation would meet with the support of the better class of citizens, and many a poor inebriate, also, would hail with joy the removal of what, to him, is an ever-present temptation.

In upholding the sale of alcoholic liquors *to be drunk off the premises*, in other places than saloons, we do so because it is always better for a man to obtain his whisky legally—since he will have it—than surreptitiously in opposition to constituted law. In legislating on this subject we must recognize the actual drinking habits of the people as they exist to-day, and not make laws for an ideal condition of society that may exist fifty or a hundred years hence. It is useless to preach temperance to an inebriate, when at the same time you hold a bludgeon in your hand to compel him to do as you wish. This is not in accordance with the Creator's plan, which leaves him the liberty of choice between good and evil and endows him with the godlike gift of reason for his guide.

If prohibitionists would dispassionately weigh the facts and conclusions contained in this work, we could confidently hope that, under wise guidance, their future efforts for the reformation of the intemperate would be crowned with success. To effect this, we are convinced that they must wholly eliminate from their policy the element of coercion, and, aided by past experience, substitute the more conciliatory principle of regulation.

> ' If thou wilt observe
> The rule of *not too much,* by temperance taught,
> In what thou eat'st and drink'st, seeking from thence
> Due nourishment, not gluttonous delight,
> Till many years over thy head return:
> So may'st thou live, till, like ripe fruit, thou drop
> Into thy mother's lap, or be with ease
> Gathered, not harshly plucked, for death mature."

www.ingramcontent.com/pod-product-compliance
Lightning Source LLC
Chambersburg PA
CBHW020109170426
43199CB00009B/462